# FOOD TRIPS

## AND TRAPS

# FOOD TRIPS AND TRAPS

## COPING WITH EATING DISORDERS

BY JANE CLAYPOOL Miner
AND
CHERYL DIANE NELSEN

A GROLIER COMPANY

FRANKLIN WATTS
NEW YORK I LONDON I TORONTO I SYDNEY I 1983

This book is dedicated to anyone who has
suffered from an eating disorder; and especially
to those who have found the courage to seek help.


Special thanks to
those who shared their personal stories openly;
to Phyllis Zack, Joan Peronto, and Ruth Degenhardt
of the Berkshire Athenaeum Staff; and
to Barbara Joslyn.


Diagrams courtesy of Anne Canevari Green

Library of Congress Cataloging in Publication Data

Claypool, Jane.
Food trips and traps.

Bibliography: p.
Includes index.
Summary: Discusses the causes of and treatments for
three harmful eating disorders: compulsive overeating,
bulimia, or the binge and purge syndrome, and anorexia
nervosa, or self-starvation.
1. Appetite disorders—Juvenile literature.
[1. Appetite disorders.   2. Food habits.   3. Obesity.
4. Bulimarexia.   5. Anorexia nervosa]
I. Nelsen, Cheryl Diane.  II. Title.
RC552.A72C52  1983          616.85′2          83-3675
ISBN 0-531-04664-8

# CONTENTS

# ONE

---

# FOOD TRIPS
# AND TRAPS

Food is essential. Without it, we couldn't continue to think, move, or breathe. Because it is so essential, it is easy to abuse. Unlike the taking of drugs or drinking of alcohol, it is never illegal for anyone to eat too much or too little. In fact, our society encourages a concern with food that goes far beyond the satisfaction of the nutritional needs of our bodies.

Most holiday and family gatherings are based on food. Birthday parties feature cake and ice cream. Thanksgiving is a feast of food sharing that originated as a celebration of bountiful crops. It is difficult to think of a holiday or special occasion that doesn't revolve around food.

Food also serves as a reward in our culture. Commercials tell us to "start our day right" by choosing a specific brand of breakfast food and to drink a special brand of soda if we want to be popular. As young children, many of us were given candy for good behavior. With such an emphasis on food, it's easy to see how some people develop problems related to it.

Nearly everyone has engaged in some kind of food "trip" at one time or another. Perhaps you skip a nourish-

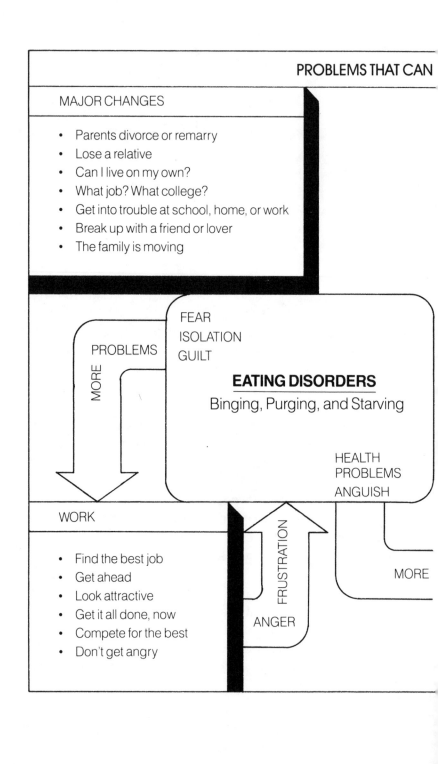

PROBLEMS THAT CAN

MAJOR CHANGES

- Parents divorce or remarry
- Lose a relative
- Can I live on my own?
- What job? What college?
- Get into trouble at school, home, or work
- Break up with a friend or lover
- The family is moving

MORE PROBLEMS

FEAR
ISOLATION
GUILT

**EATING DISORDERS**

Binging, Purging, and Starving

HEALTH
PROBLEMS
ANGUISH

WORK

- Find the best job
- Get ahead
- Look attractive
- Get it all done, now
- Compete for the best
- Don't get angry

FRUSTRATION

ANGER

MORE

# CAUSE EATING DISORDERS

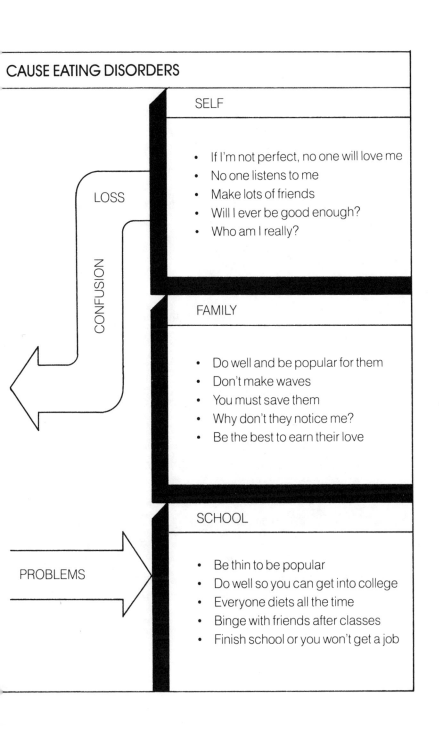

**SELF**

- If I'm not perfect, no one will love me
- No one listens to me
- Make lots of friends
- Will I ever be good enough?
- Who am I really?

LOSS

CONFUSION

**FAMILY**

- Do well and be popular for them
- Don't make waves
- You must save them
- Why don't they notice me?
- Be the best to earn their love

PROBLEMS

**SCHOOL**

- Be thin to be popular
- Do well so you can get into college
- Everyone diets all the time
- Binge with friends after classes
- Finish school or you won't get a job

ing meal at home and then go out with friends to binge on hot dogs, french fries, and a milk shake. Or perhaps you get a huge container of buttered popcorn at the movies even though you are a few pounds overweight. Slightly erratic eating patterns are common among teenagers. As your body matures, you may crave certain foods. Sometimes only a few junk or health foods appeal to you. This is normal, and not harmful, as long as you are sure to eat a variety of foods so that your body gets the vitamins and minerals it needs.

## WHEN FOOD BECOMES A PROBLEM

*I didn't want all those calories in my body . . . I was obsessed and I felt like it was my own private little "trip."*
>Eileen, talking about her
>problems with anorexia and bulimia

*I would consume too much one day and not eat for the next couple of days. Food was no longer a normal part of my life but something I had to put the brakes on.*
>Samantha, talking about her
>compulsive eating

*The period of my life when I suffered from anorexia was certainly the time I felt the most inconsequential. I felt like no one was hearing me—no one.*
>Beth, a compulsive eater,
>talking about the
>anorectic period of her life

Food has been a serious problem in the lives of these three women. Only Samantha now feels she has control over her compulsive eating. Eileen and Beth have been working on their problems, and improving. Unlike the food "trips" most people experience, food has become a trap for these women and for thousands of other people.

Food can become a trap when it is used as a substitute for love, friendship, or success; or when it is used to cover up more serious emotional conflicts. Craving the food in the refrigerator when one is full or avoiding food to the point of starvation are symptoms of serious underlying problems. Some people just can't stop eating once they start. When bored or under stress, some people binge, consuming everything they can find, and then purge by vomiting or using medicine. Still others start a diet with good intentions, then become obsessed with it, and turn into starving, frail skeletons. These food traps—compulsive eating, bulimia, and anorexia nervosa—are often combined or alternated. They can ruin a person's health and cause a great deal of guilt, suffering, and anguish. They can even result in death.

## WHEN YOU KEEP EATING

*Compulsive eating* is an uncontrolled consumption of vast amounts of food not based on hunger. Compulsive eaters eat past the point of full stomachs and sometimes even past the point of nausea. They may consume a whole pie, a large container of ice cream, and several delicatessen sandwiches, and then lick clean a jar of peanut butter. They may go to several restaurants, one right after another, and have a meal at each, or empty the entire refrigerator.

The occasional "pig-out" or "attack of the munchies" which results in a midnight pizza snack or a visit to an ice cream parlor is a mild form of compulsive eating that is not something to worry about. When most people indulge their food cravings, they stop eating when they feel full. This is not the case with truly compulsive eaters. They keep eating past the full feeling that stops most of us. There is no absolute boundary line between normal eating and compulsive eating, but reliable indicators are the amount of food eaten and the amount of time and money spent on food.

Although some mild compulsive eating occurs in groups, the more serious kind is often a very lonely enterprise. Food may be hidden, purchased in secret, or even stolen. One compulsive eater claims she eats only in her car, especially when she is driving home to her empty house. Another admits she stocks up on a variety of rich desserts, tells herself that they are for company, and then eats them all before she gets home. Some compulsive eaters may eat very little in front of others in order to get sympathy for their evident control, and then binge in secret later. One reason compulsive eaters often keep their overeating a secret is that they fear the shock and disapproval that they might get from their friends and family if they were discovered. They eat to find solace from stress and from their problems. If others knew about the extent of their eating, compulsive eaters might suffer from even more stress and guilt.

Other compulsive eaters aren't so secretive. Their overeating is a way to protest against a lack of attention from family and friends. These compulsive eaters sometimes flaunt their uncontrolled eating habits by bragging about the amount of food they can eat or the high quality of the gourmet meals they consume.

Compulsive eating is often a smoke screen, a cover-up for more serious problems. The compulsive eater may feel unable to communicate with others. She may not have a sense of belonging. He may be unable to act out wishes, dreams, or desires. In some cases, eating may seem like the only relief for the dilemmas they face.

Sometimes compulsive eating can serve as a warning of serious underlying problems. Dr. Albert Stunkard, in his book, *I Almost Feel Thin!*, discusses the positive side of compulsive eating binges: "The binges themselves may even be an asset, for an understanding of the events which cause eating binges frequently leads directly to the major conflicts which disturb the patient."

These major conflicts may be deep-rooted and complex. If brought to light without professional help, these hidden conflicts can cause other, sometimes worse problems. When exploring the serious conflicts behind compulsive eating, it is important to get help from a psychiatrist, psychologist, or other therapist who is specially trained and experienced in dealing with eating disorders.

## THE BINGE AND PURGE SYNDROME

When binges of compulsive eating are combined with extended fasting, vomiting, or the use of medicines to rid the body of food consumed, the term *bulimia* is applied. Bulimia comes from two Greek words, "bous," meaning cow or ox, and "limos," meaning hunger or famine. *Time* magazine recently reported that some bulimics gorge up to five times per week, consuming 40,000 calories and taking as many as 600 laxative pills. Other bulimics admit to daily binges and vomiting. Still others purge after nearly every meal and snack, and claim they feel bloated and fat whatever and whenever they eat. Many compulsive eaters become bulimic in hopes of gaining relief from the guilt and bloatedness of overeating.

Bulimia has recently reached epidemic proportions.

According to studies on college campuses in the late seventies, 15 to 30 percent of the women questioned had engaged in some form of binging and purging. Dr. William Davis, the director of the Center for the Study of Anorexia and Bulimia in New York City, estimated in 1981 that more than 5 percent of the adult women in the United States may be bulimic. It is difficult to estimate how many bulimics there really are because many are still horrified by their disease, while others don't realize that it is a serious problem, and therefore both groups don't report their illness. Recent publicity has caused thousands of women suffering from this syndrome to write to regional centers that research and treat bulimia. Unfortunately, the publicity has also caused some people to try binging and purging for the first time.

Nearly all known bulimics are women, although some cases have been found in men, especially among those in professions such as dancing, jockeying, and wrestling, for which slimness is important. A majority of bulimics are in their twenties and thirties; some are successful career women, others ambitious college students. However, the victims of the disease range from teenagers to grandmothers. Recently, many older bulimics have sought help after decades of binging and purging.

Many bulimics report that they first saw purging as the magic solution to their struggles for weight control. Movie star Jane Fonda, a reformed bulimic, remembers when she and her friends discovered bulimia at boarding school. They thought, "Here's the way to *not* have our cake and eat it too!"

Thousands of other bulimics have also thought that they had found the painless cure for overeating. They did not realize that their solution was neither painless nor a cure. First of all, purging cannot cause the stored fat on a person's body to be lost, except in cases of extreme starvation. Secondly, the purging creates new cravings which cause more binging and purging. Soon bulimia has taken over, and the bulimic must spend much of her time and money satisfying the demands of the disease.

There are serious medical consequences also. Not all the sugars of rich foods are purged from the body. Some sugar remains to damage teeth. Abuse of laxatives and diuretics, medicines used by bulimics to rid their bodies of food and liquids, also cause the body to eliminate its needed salts, potassium and magnesium. This can lead to serious, sometimes fatal, imbalances in the body's electrolyte system. Fasting causes the body to draw its needed energy from organs and muscle tissue. While these break down to supply the body's needs, fluids, vitamins, and minerals are lost. Vomiting causes similiar problems as well as damage to the lining of the throat, esophagus, and stomach. In extreme cases, the lining of the esophagus ruptures and causes death.

**THE STARVATION SICKNESS**
At first, bulimia was considered one of the symptoms of *anorexia nervosa*, the starvation disease. Anorexia nervosa literally means a nervous condition producing loss of appetite. But the name is misleading. Anorectics are self-starvers who consciously choose to ignore their hunger and consequently can waste away to skeletons. Some anorectics do alternate their starvation with binging and purging. Others simply refuse to eat.

Sometimes, anorexia starts with a rigidly enforced diet. Maybe someone has teased the future anorectic about being "chubby," or perhaps she has failed an important test in school. Seemingly minor triggering incidents like these often set the anorectic on her collision course with this potentially fatal illness. She initially loses a few pounds easily. Then she can't stop. She exercises frantically and refuses to eat much. She may divide her food in strange ways, hide it, or just pretend to eat. Her behavior after weeks of self-induced starvation begins to resemble that of a concentration camp survivor. She may dream of food constantly and develop complex mental patterns. After a few months, she has lost 25 percent or more of her weight and completely withdrawn as a result of her starvation.

It was once thought that anorexia was a symptom associated only with complex and severe mental problems. In some cases of anorectic-like behavior in mental patients, this is true. But anorexia nervosa is no longer simply a label for the component of emotional illness that involves refusal to eat. It is now seen as a distinct set of behavioral and physical problems. These include denial of starvation, hyperactivity—at least at the beginning, before the body's resources are depleted—a distorted sense of body image, and withdrawal from friends and family. The physical manifestations include loss of menstrual periods, increased sensitivity to heat and cold, pale skin, hair loss combined with the development of downy hair all over the body, and obvious emaciation with ribs and hipbones showing.

Theories about the cause of anorexia have often been physiological in nature. The disorder has been attributed to nutritional imbalances, brain malfunction, and hormonal problems. But these theories remain unproven. Although there are cases of starvation due to medical causes, they are rare, and most victims of these disorders do not display the same mental characteristics that anorectics do.

Most experts currently agree that starvation can bring on or aggravate the cluster of mental characteristics associated with anorexia, but that no direct physical causes for the disease have been sufficiently proven.

What, then, causes a young woman to voluntarily starve herself to death? One theory is that some girls, when maturing into womanhood, may be too frightened to face the changes taking place in their bodies and in their lives. Another theory states that the anorectic's family has pressured her to be the best in everything, but the only thing she feels she can truly control is her own body. Society's pressure to be thin and glamorous and to count calories can be taken to extremes and lead to starvation. Often, it is a combination of pressures that causes the anorectic to starve herself.

These pressures may trouble the victim long before she refuses to eat. Anorectics often withdraw from their families and friends and become preoccupied with food for as much as a year or two before they stop eating. Unfortunately, it is difficult to identify those who are developing anorexia. Many of their habits are part of many normal teenagers' lives. In addition, both criticism and concern from others can cause the anorectic's problems to worsen. If told to eat, she may withdraw even further from her parents. If friends show concern, it may be misinterpreted as rejection.

## HELPING ANORECTICS
## AND BULIMICS
Professionals, parents, and recovering anorectics and bulimics have banded together and formed aid groups in many parts of the country. These groups offer detailed information to victims, and refer them to therapists and

doctors. They often sponsor sessions to help both the patients and their families cope with the ramifications of the disease.

There are now several major research centers at hospitals and universities that are engaged in the study and treatment of bulimia and anorexia. Although experts still cannot guarantee a speedy recovery, most say it is difficult but possible to recover totally from a serious eating disorder.

If you or someone you care about needs help, check the list at the back of this book and contact the nearest group for advice and referrals. Urge the person who is purging or starving to consult a competent internist and to report what has been occurring. This is important for the treatment of any serious physical problems that may have developed. But getting help from a qualified therapist who has had experience in this very specialized area is just as important.

## WHY WOMEN?

The majority of compulsive eaters seen in treatment are women. Statistics show that 90 to 95 percent of those suffering from anorexia are female. Reports indicate that nearly all bulimics are women, too. Are there special pressures that cause women to have eating disorders?

Many experts say yes. Traditionally, men have been encouraged to express their anger openly and to make decisions about their own lives, while women have been taught to suppress their anger, be passive, and rely on others for their needs. However, one major area in which women have nearly always been in charge is food. Some women may turn to food or away from it to find escape from their problems.

In our currently changing society, women are now expected to compete with men at school and on the job. Yet many of these same women are urged to be sweet and passive in their relationships with boyfriends and husbands. Their dilemma has been labeled "a double bind." It has been suggested that this modern-day conflict leads even more women to seek solace in food than the more traditional situation did. Others seek relief from this double bind by refusing to eat at all.

Women are faced with another conflict when they watch television and read magazines. They see countless tempting recipes and commercials about rich, caloric food. Yet they are also presented with a multitude of diets and are surrounded by images of beautiful, thin women. They are being encouraged to concern themselves with rich foods, yet they are told that they must be slim if they want to be desirable.

The "ideal" woman has not always been as skinny as today's successful models. In past centuries, famous paintings and sculptures showed women with large breasts and hips and full faces. At the beginning of this century, "The Gibson Girl," a large, fully-developed woman, was the ideal model. By current standards, Marilyn Monroe, the shapely blond superstar of the fifties, would be considered fat. A recent study of a popular men's magazine showed that each year, for the past twenty years, their featured photos were of thinner and smaller women.

Why is the ideal woman's shape shrinking? Some experts claim that because highly developed countries like the United States have enough food, fat is no longer a status symbol. Others suggest that men don't want to compete on the job with large women; they seem to find small women less of a threat. Still others say that the women themselves want to escape the old-fashioned, passive image that may be associated with being amply built. Whatever the reasons, being thin enough to be considered beautiful is a constant challenge for women, a challenge that sometimes leads to serious food abuse.

## THE WARNING SIGNS

It is sometimes impossible to know for certain if you or someone you care about is suffering from a serious eating disorder. If *several* of the following warning signs are present, you should get professional help to make a diagnosis. A list of referral and information centers and groups appears at the back of this book.

## COMPULSIVE EATING

*(See also Bulimia.)*

- inability to stop eating when physically full
- eating after meals or when not really hungry
- eating when bored, frustrated, or nervous
- eating entire packages of food or several portions, without really even tasting it
- eating to celebrate every minor victory and recover from every minor defeat
- spending a lot of money on sweets, junk food, or health food not eaten at meals or meant to be shared with others
- shopping for and eating food secretly
- stealing food or money with which to buy it
- guilt from constantly eating too much

## BULIMIA

*(See also Compulsive Eating and Anorexia.)*

- food binges followed by vomiting, fasting, or use of laxatives, enemas, and/or diuretics

- inability to eat without purging
- fear of not being able to control eating
- constant fear of being fat although weight is within a 15-pound (7-kg) range of what is considered normal for your age and height
- irregular menstrual periods
- extreme tooth decay
- swollen salivary glands, body cramps, and dizziness
- significant weight changes

## ANOREXIA
*(See also Compulsive Eating and Bulimia.)*
- weight loss of 25 percent or more
- feeling that a diet has taken over
- food seen as an enemy
- consuming less than 600 calories per day on a regular basis
- rushing from the table to vomit after being forced to eat
- alternating compulsive eating and bulimia with significant periods of starvation
- taking hours to prepare elaborate food for others, then not eating any or much yourself
- shopping for or demanding that others shop for special gourmet foods, and then not eating them
- withdrawal from friends and family
- constant exercise
- loss of menstrual periods
- pacing around while eating
- a distorted body image, claiming to be fat though much weight has been lost
- a new layer of fine, downy hair covering body
- bruises from unpadded bones
- infections that don't heal

- sunken eyes
- grey or yellowed skin, sometimes broken out
- patchy, dry head hair
- hiding or flaunting emaciated shape
- decreased ability to tolerate cold temperatures
- significant insomnia
- increased depression and irritability

# TWO

## WHEN YOU CAN'T STOP

Compulsive eaters are out of control. Theirs is not the occasional overeating many of us experience. They force food into their mouths at alarming rates. They don't stop at the point of fullness. Theirs is a seemingly insatiable hunger.

After exercise or a skipped meal most people feel ravenous, ready to eat more than usual. But compulsive eating isn't motivated by a simple hunger for food. Instead, it stems from complex emotional causes that are not completely understood. Compulsive eating is one way many people deal with stress, frustration, and even the fear of success. Though there can be malfunctions in the body that cause overeating, these cases are rare.

There are numerous stories and jokes about seemingly jolly, fat people and their struggles with food. Some of the stories compulsive eaters tell about their battles to keep from eating are funny, at first. One young businesswoman has a huge chain and lock on her refrigerator. Her neighbor keeps the key. A sixteen-year-old girl has written, "Stay away! Poison!!" across an elephant's picture, and posted it on the pantry door that opens to her favorite binging sweets.

But the facts aren't funny. Many overweight people are depressed and frustrated. Dealing with "fat jokes" can make their situation even more difficult. In its mild form, compulsive eating may mean an occasional indulgence. In extreme cases, people's whole lives revolve around food and the guilt they feel for eating too much. Some compulsive eaters gain over 100 pounds (45 kg) in a few months. Others develop bulimic and anorexic tendencies and interrupt their binging with periods of purging and fasting.

## LAURA'S SUGAR BINGES

As long as Laura can remember, she has had a sweet tooth. Lately, though, things seem to be getting out of hand. She goes on an ice cream binge two or three times a week. It starts with a trip to the supermarket for her favorite brand, a rich half-gallon of mocha fudge ripple. She eats a bowl, telling herself that it should be enough. Then she dips her spoon in the box and finishes it. Soon it's time for dinner. She piles as much food as she can onto her plate. She also snacks later while she watches television or does homework.

Her parents have noticed the 20 pounds (9 kg) she has recently put on. Her mother is concerned, but says, "Well, at least, she's not into drugs or booze. She'll outgrow it."

Laura's compulsive eating does seem mild when compared to the horror stories of other compulsive eaters. Still, she is out of control. Her casual binging is no longer a simple sweet tooth treat. She may outgrow it, just as her mother predicts, or it may lead to other problems. Some compulsive eaters also abuse drugs and alcohol. Other people's food disorders eventually take over their personalities.

If Laura is able to gain some comfort from food while dealing with the frustrations of life that cause her to overeat, she may, indeed, outgrow her mild problem. She may seek help from a group like Weight Watchers or Overeaters Anonymous. Or she may find she needs the help of a therapist. But it is important that she get help early. Experts have found that the earlier someone gets help, the better chance they have of solving their eating problems before the illness takes over their lives.

## HOW IT ALL STARTED

Unlike Laura, Fran does remember the first time she had a problem with compulsive eating. She wasn't always interested in food. As an unhappy child, food was the last thing she had considered turning to for comfort. At thirteen, when she was in the eighth grade, both of her older brothers left home. She had looked up to them and had turned to them for support and encouragement. Fran recalls the first time she lost control with food. It launched her on a twenty-year battle to keep her weight down.

> I attended a slumber party where there were a lot of goodies to eat. It's possible we'd been talking about guys. I remember eating a lot of cookies, but particularly chocolate bar after chocolate bar, and not being able to stop.

> I thought at the time, "That's okay. You can get as fat and as full as you want. You don't have to keep eating like this tomorrow."

> From that point on, I had to struggle.

Fran continued to binge. It was hard for her to face the quiet home where her older brothers and their friends had been. Instead of making new friends herself or trying to confide in her parents, Fran found it easier to "hit the ice-box."

When Fran tried to work on her problem by dieting and eating less, she grew more depressed and frustrated. Then she began to eat more, and gained more weight. Such a rebound after dieting is common, especially for those compulsive eaters whose obsession with food is making up for something lacking in their lives.

## DIETING AND
## THE COMPULSIVE EATER

Many experts feel that dieting is not the solution to compulsive eating. Dr. Jean Mayer, an authority on nutrition, writes in his book, *Overweight: Causes, Cost and Control:* "If grief and lack of affection, success or popularity are involved, harm may be done by superimposing the discomfort of food restrictions on a situation already difficult enough. In such cases, food deprivation may make emotional problems even more severe."

Instead of helping, dieting can turn the compulsive eater into a compulsive dieter. It can also set the dieter up for one more disappointment. If she breaks the diet or doesn't reach her goal, she sees herself as a failure. If she reaches her weight goal and her life doesn't suddenly change dramatically, she still feels like a failure. Strict diets can also lead to bulimia and anorexia. The pressures from dieting can cause more problems than they cure.

What, then, is the answer? Diet sensibly and allow yourself some pleasure from food. If you think your eating problem has underlying emotional causes, get professional help or join a support group where you can talk about your problems openly. And, above all, remember that losing weight or controlling your eating won't instantly solve all your problems.

## GROUP BINGES

Many compulsive eaters get started while eating in groups. Friends and co-workers can give a compulsive eater an excuse to eat, and, frequently, to overeat. Because eating with others is seen as a special occasion, it is all right to go overboard. Other people with eating problems may even encourage friends to overeat, so that they feel better about their own eating habits.

There is nothing wrong with eating with friends. It can be a relaxing and important part of friendship and a way to get to know people better. But when a friendship or group centers exclusively on food, something may be wrong. There are two choices for a compulsive eater involved in a friendship or group obsessed with food: change the focus of the group or leave it. The focus can be changed by doing other activities together, such as sports, movies, or shopping trips.

## SECRET EATING

Although some compulsive eating occurs in groups, many compulsive eaters with serious problems hide their behavior from others so that they don't have to face criticism. They may even get sympathy if they have a weight problem.

Arnold comes from a family of big eaters. His mother serves the family huge meals and his father brags about how much he can eat. Arnold does well in school but doesn't like gym class because he worries about what others think when they see his 200-pound (100-kg) body exercising.

He pretends to be the perfect dieter. He refuses the large breakfast his mother offers, taking only toast, juice, and skim milk. On the way to school he detours to the store in the next neighborhood and stocks up on chips, cheese crackers, and the beef jerky he loves to chew. At lunch he buys milk and one sandwich, and forces himself to leave half the sandwich on the tray. His friends say, "It's a shame you can't lose weight. You eat so little." Arnold answers, "Fat runs in my family, there's no way to shake it."

After his public performance, Arnold visits his locker to binge on the foods he bought before school. When school ends, he treats himself to a pizza, a quart of root beer, and an assortment of candy bars. Still unsatisfied, he buys a cheesecake at a delicatessen "to take home to his mother." It never arrives.

Arnold continues to eat in secret late at night after eating very little for dinner. By deceiving those around him, Arnold gets a great deal of sympathy for being overweight. He can also pretend to be in control, at least at formal mealtimes. Still, he feels guilty about his secret. He needs both the support of his parents and professional help.

## A NIGHTMARE OF
## COMPULSIVE EATING

A tragic but true story is told by a compulsive eater's sister, Diane Broughton, in the book, *Confessions of A Compulsive Eater*. Broughton's sister, Cam, was a problem eater whose sugar binges, diet pill dependence, and health problems led to her death in 1981.

Cam's food games started with childhood charge accounts with the ice-cream vender and frequent eating out. As an adult she raided fast-food franchises. Her life was one continuous food binge interrupted by occasional fasts. Because of her dieting, she was never seriously overweight. At one point, she only weighed 101 pounds (45 kg), although she was 5 feet 7 inches (1.5 m). Being pretty and thin were as important to her as her food binges. Today, Cam would probably be called bulimic, because her eating binges were alternated with fasts.

Her doctors didn't focus on her eating problems. When she was twenty-two, they diagnosed her as a diabetic. She needed insulin shots daily, but wouldn't take them when she feared they would cause weight gain. She had to have a reasonable amount of food in her stomach to take the shots, but for her no amount was reasonable.

Cam's sister says that Cam tried every cure she could find for her problems. Unfortunately, she tried two very dangerous ones, fasting and diet pills. Cam's body couldn't take the strain accumulated from her many years of binging, fasting, and taking diet pills. Cam was able to overcome her addiction to the pills, but she couldn't stop eating. Finally, the strain proved too much. She lost her sight and suffered kidney and other internal organ damage, and developed serious infections. These and the long years of abuse led to her death.

Cam's story is a nightmare. It is an extreme case of compulsive eating. Cam's habits took over her life and then claimed it.

# THREE

## COMPULSIVE EATING: CAUSES AND CURES

What causes a compulsive eater to ravenously consume whole packages of cookies, more than one pizza, and then every pickle in the jar? Some researchers claim that hunger triggers in the brain aren't working correctly. Others point to certain kinds of food that cause chemical reactions that lead to more compulsive eating. Still others insist that compulsive eating is a reawakening of primitive survival instincts from early days when humans hunted for their food. Many experts see it as a mask or cover-up for other, deeper problems.

Which of these theories is correct? Each has been proposed and then called into question by further research; most of the theories are difficult to prove or disprove. Rather than trying to find a single cause, many doctors and researchers see the problem as having many causes. They believe each case is unique, as is each person involved. Still, some patterns recur in many compulsive eaters, and they can be evaluated.

Dr. Hilde Bruch, one of the foremost experts in this area, points out in her book, *Eating Disorders,* that "various different symptom complexes which cannot be explained by one simple mechanism'' are at work. She suggests that eating disorders spring not just from the body's chemistry or the person's emotions, but rather from a combination, ''an expression of disturbances in the interaction of these various forces.'' As we look at some of the different theories about the causes of overeating, keep in mind that many complex factors may be involved in any one case.

## BRAIN CONTROLS
## ON HUNGER

Until recently, the brain was believed to be divided into specific areas, each of which controlled certain functions, such as thought, memory, actions, and emotional responses. The part of the brain thought to be responsible for eating was the *hypothalamus.* This part of the brain was also believed to be responsible for regulating body temperature, and for other necessary functions that are called ''involuntary'' because they occur without people's awareness of them. As the list of involuntary actions controlled by the hypothalamus grew, scientists began to believe there were two triggers that regulated hunger. One signaled the need to eat. Another stopped the eating process when the body was full. The second trigger was believed to signal satiety—the full feeling experienced when the body has consumed all the food it needs.

Research with laboratory rats showed that when the hypothalamus was tampered with surgically, they became overeaters. At first, this was thought to prove that the brain does control appetite. Later research showed that the same operation caused rats to stop exercising, too. Although these findings are fascinating, the studies of rats with severely altered brains do not have enough direct bearing on humans who overeat to prove conclusively that overeating is controlled by the brain. Recently, scientists have explored the theory that triggers for hunger as well as for other involuntary functions are found in different parts of the brain rather than in specific areas, and that the brain works as a whole system of interacting functions.

## CHEMICAL IMBALANCES

Many theories link compulsive eating and weight gain to chemical imbalances in the body. One possibility is that the processed sugars, flours, and chemical additives in many junk foods and sweets lead to additional food abuse. Another theory blames imbalances in the body that falsely trigger the brain to desire more food when the body is actually satiated. These imbalances may be found in blood sugars, enzymes, and other necessary elements in the digestion and utilization of food. Allergies to certain foods are also seen as responsible for the chemical imbalances that trigger compulsive eating.

Some compulsive eaters use imagined physical problems as an excuse for their food disorder. Others do have physical problems that lead to or aggravate their problems with food. Chemical imbalances exist in many long-term compulsive eaters. It is difficult to prove, however, whether their physical abnormalities led to food abuse or were caused by it.

## BACK TO THE CAVE

The earliest humans hunted and searched for their food. Winter was often a time of famine because there were few animals about and no berries or nuts to be foraged. Humans also starved in times of drought and during other natural disasters.

When food was available, it had to be eaten quickly. There was no refrigeration and little was known about cooking and storing food. Humans had to store fat on their bodies for the lean times when they had nothing to eat.

Could compulsive eating be a throwback to early times when people had to eat everything in sight just to stay alive? A few experts believe this is one possible factor that triggers compulsive eating.

## FAMILY FACTORS

The family history of a person can influence the amount he or she eats. Like many traits, one's appetite and the tendency to overeat may be inherited from one's parents. If a person's ancestors were from a cold climate and needed a layer of fat to protect them, this tendency may have been passed on to new generations living in a different climate. Sometimes, only those possessing the necessary fat layer survived long enough to produce offspring. If one's ancestors labored vigorously in the fields or walked miles each day, a hearty appetite might have been necessary to make sure they got enough nourishment for their active lives. When this huge appetite is passed on to modern generations which don't work as hard physically or need as much food, problems can arise. Each person has inherited a different degree of appetite and a different body build.

The family's attitude toward food is also an important factor. Some experts believe that overfeeding young children causes them to overeat later in life. If the family is too concerned with eating or dieting, this concern can cause anxiety which may trigger compulsive eating. If a person has had food withheld from or forced upon him or her, this, too, can lead to food abuse.

## FOOD MEANS LOVE

Food is often used as a substitute for love, attention, and pampering. When people are not around to give attention to the compulsive eater, food can provide comfort. "Love-starved" is an old expression, but it explains the compulsive eater's need for food. The comforting, exciting feeling of putting nourishment in one's mouth starts as a baby. Traditional psychiatry refers to this sensation as "oral gratification." Many experts believe that the pleasure and contentment that come from filling one's mouth with food can be a substitute for sexual fulfillment. This may explain why many compulsive eaters say they don't really care what type of food they eat, as long as they get enough of it into their mouths and stomachs. They crave the full, satisfied sensation that makes them feel better about the rest of their lives.

## FOOD MEANS POWER

As children, we do not control our food intake; our parents are responsible for feeding us. As we grow older, we make decisions about when and what to eat. Some compulsive eaters feel they are exercising considerable power by eating all the food they can find. Sometimes, it is the only power they feel they have in their lives.

On the other hand, some people feel totally powerless around food. They see food as an enemy that is controlling their entire lives. By seeing food in this way, they feel they don't have to control their eating. After all, if food is in control, there is no possible way to win. This frees compulsive eaters to eat more.

## GETTING CONTROL
## OVER COMPULSIVE EATING

Just as there are numerous possible causes of compulsive eating, there are many different cures. What really helps or hurts a recovery are the amount of time and energy a person is willing to spend, the amount of willpower and stamina he or she can muster, and the willingness to follow through on a plan of action. Many compulsive eaters, especially those who have had a long-term problem, need professional help in order to conquer their problem. Others can find help through support groups, and some even win their battle over food abuse by themselves.

## MONITORING
## EATING PATTERNS
A good first step, especially in mild cases of compulsive eating, is to look at the patterns of where, when, and how much the compulsive eater indulges. This can provide clues as to the reasons that a person overeats, and if a record is kept by the compulsive eater, he or she may gain some feeling of control over food intake. A chart should include the following categories: Time of Day, Food Eaten, Thoughts, Events, and Feelings. If a chart seems difficult to set up, an alternative is to keep a journal of one's eating habits, jotting down notes about experiences as they happen, or at a certain time each day.

By keeping a chart or journal, the compulsive eater is able to think before eating and review his or her eating behavior after it occurs. This valuable information can be, used in group or individual therapy, too.

## PLANNING BINGES
It may seem unusual, but binges can be planned and sometimes limited. Many compulsive eaters have had success by gradually limiting their binges, to eliminate the panic that quitting altogether can cause. Scheduling and allowing certain indulgences reduces guilt and anxiety, and gives the compulsive eater a feeling of power over eating. Food is seen less as an undefeatable enemy and more as a substance that can be controlled. By limiting and planning,

many compulsive eaters have found that they crave fewer binges.

## GETTING HELP FROM OTHERS

Compulsive eating often cannot be faced alone. Because it is a problem for so many people, help is widely available in the form of medical treatment, support groups, and individual and family therapy. Some treatments can be expensive, while others are priced with sliding scales to allow people with different incomes to get help.

## FIRST, RULE OUT
## PHYSICAL CAUSES

A comprehensive medical examination to evaluate the body's condition is the best first step. A physical examination may uncover imbalances or other medical problems caused by overeating; or it may uncover physical conditions that helped to cause the overeating in the first place. If the person has been purging, fasting, or using medicines, an internist with experience in treating eating disorders should be consulted. Otherwise, it is best to consult with a family physician, a clinic specializing in weight or eating disorders, or doctors who have had experience treating compulsive eaters. If any doctor or clinic minimizes or takes the problems of a compulsive eater too lightly, a different one should be consulted.

## SELF-HELP GROUPS

These range from diet groups like Overeaters Anonymous and Weight Watchers to groups led by therapists and eating disorder clinics. Compulsive eaters are often helped by knowing that they are not alone and by learning about tactics that have worked for other people. There is sometimes a wonderful release in sharing problems with others who understand because they have been there, too.

The groups in a compulsive eater's geographical area can be found by checking the yellow pages, consulting with a local mental health association, or contacting the organizations in the back of this book for referrals.

## THERAPY

Many compulsive eaters have benefited from exploring the emotional factors that helped to cause their eating binges. Besides group therapy, individual help from a psychiatrist, psychologist, or psychiatric social worker may be the answer. A few years ago, there were few options for the treatment of people with eating problems. Some therapists did not feel that eating problems were serious enough for treatment. This has changed over the past few years. Therapists now offer a range of techniques to help the compulsive eater, from traditional methods to hypnosis and meditation therapies. Not every treatment or therapist is effective for every compulsive eater. It is important to find a therapist you can trust and a technique you think may work for you.

When choosing a therapist, consider the following:

(1) You will not be cured magically or overnight. The reasons for compulsive eating can be complex.

(2) Look for someone with whom you feel comfortable and who you really believe can help you.

(3) Don't rely entirely on the therapist. In most cases, you will have to do much of the work yourself in order to achieve success.

(4) Seek out a professional with a great deal of experience treating compulsive eaters. If you can, talk with the therapist's current and former patients. Try to get several opinions.

(5) Consider changing professionals if treatment doesn't help after several weeks or months, or if your problems aren't taken seriously enough.

# FOUR

## BULIMIA:
## THE BINGE AND PURGE
## SYNDROME

Bulimia wasn't recognized as a separate, distinct eating disorder until the early 1980s. It used to be considered a symptom of anorexia nervosa, the starvation sickness. Many anorectics do binge and purge at times. Many more people, perhaps ten times as many, binge and purge without becoming anorectic. Because of their normal weight and secretive behavior, bulimics often go undetected.

Most bulimics are women. Unlike anorectics, who are often "perfect little girls" having trouble growing up, bulimics are usually older and are often involved in successful careers or in doing well at competitive colleges. Some therapists see them as outgoing women whose lives may include relationships with men. Sometimes bulimics also abuse alcohol and drugs.

Instead of refusing to eat, the bulimic binges on 1,000 to 20,000 calories at a time. The latter figure can be as much as ten times the normal daily caloric intake of a woman. The binge foods are mostly sweets and starches. The bulimic then fasts. Or, she purges by self-induced vomiting, and/or using laxatives, diuretics, and enemas. At first, she may purge to feel relief from the guilt of binging and the fear of weight gain. Later, purging can take control and become more important than binging. When the ritual aspect has taken over a woman's life, she may eat only so that she can purge, saying it makes her feel pure and free to rid herself of the consumed food. Or she may not be able to eat without purging because panic and fear take over as she swallows.

## A CHANGE OF SCENE
Eileen had been troubled by anorectic tendencies in high school. Despite her severe diet and other personal problems, she was an honor-roll student and got a scholarship to one of the country's best women's colleges. Her bulimia became serious after she left home:

> When I got to college, it was a whole change of scene and I started gaining weight. I met this woman who was a vegetarian. She was an inspiration to me. I quit eating meat and ate lots of fruits and vegetables but no dairy products, grains, or nuts.
>
> I'd start craving sugar and get a whole bunch of candy bars—all kinds—or eat honey or a whole bunch of nuts—just eat, eat, eat, eat, and eat. Then, all of a sudden, I'd realize I didn't want all those calories in my body.
>
> I'd think, "I can't gain weight!" I'd take a herbal laxative and make myself throw up.

Soon, Eileen was purging even after her vegetarian meals, and then after eating anything at all. Although she learned to purge to rid herself of unwanted food at college, she had begun alternating binges with fasting in high school. The change of scene when she left for college was just another trigger that aggravated her problems with food. Eileen is one of the many women who have suffered from a combination of anorexia and bulimia. Experts estimate that as may as half of the known anorectics later become bulimic.

## KEEPING IT SECRET

Purging practices are seen as disgusting by most people. So, the bulimic often feels a need to be secretive about her binging and purging. This only adds guilt and shame to her other frustrations. One therapist says it often takes two months to two years for her patients to feel comfortable enough to talk about their eating patterns.

Although Eileen has gotten therapy for her emotional problems at many periods of her life and has consulted doctors about her problems with food allergies and sugar levels—problems often associated with bulimia—she has never told a single doctor or therapist about her binging and purging. She considers them just habits, not important enough to mention. Yet, she also admits that she's often been terrified by her food abuse.

Unlike Eileen, many bulimics with up to decades of food abuse are now getting help. Publicity about bulimia in recent magazine articles has brought to the regional centers pleas for help from thousands of victims. As one bulimic wrote, "It's good to know I'm not just some lone freak, that there are others I can talk to about it."

In the 1960s, when Eileen was growing up, a family doctor practicing in a small town might have seen few cases of anorexia in his or her lifetime. Because bulimia was not known as a separate eating disorder with distinct behaviors and problems, the doctor might not have known how to best treat it. He or she may have referred to it as a "rare" or "strange" problem. This probably would have caused the bulimic to feel even more stressed and isolated.

Now, research centers and hospitals are training both doctors and therapists to deal with bulimia and other eating disorders. There are specialists in many parts of the country who have had first-hand experience with food abuse patients. Many have had years of experience in studying and testing cures. If Eileen still needed help today, her chances of recovery would be far better than they were in the 1960s when her problems were not widely understood.

## THE GLAMOROUS DISEASE

Being glamorous in our society means being thin and having a perfect body size. What is considered perfect is the youthful body of a not-completely-developed adolescent. This means that the normal body of an adult woman with its fully developed breasts, thighs, and hips is not seen as attractive or glamorous. This popular, if curious, attitude affects everyone who wants to look alluring or even healthy. Especially affected are people working in the arts as dancers, actresses, and actors, as well as people in other highly visible fields such as politics and sports. The small percentage of bulimics who are male, probably less than 10 percent, are thought to be mostly from the professions of acting, dancing, jockeying, and wrestling, where weight gain critically affects their eligibility, performance, or image. Anyone who appears on television looks 10 pounds (4 kg) heavier than they really are.

Many people in glamorous jobs achieve the lower-than-normal weight through vigorous exercise, seasonal retreats to health spas, and/or rigorous dieting. A few adopt the bulimic practices of gorging and purging. Since their public image is important, they must be especially secretive about this distasteful and embarrassing problem.

## ONE STAR'S FIGHT WITH BULIMIA

Jane Fonda, a well-known actress, has recently revealed her struggle with bulimia. In an interview on the television news show, "20/20," and in her best-selling *Workout Book,* she has told about her own binging and purging, which began in boarding school:

> *I remember one year when we studied Roman civilization, we came across a footnote explaining how the Romans made a practice of retreating to a room known as the vomitorium during their orgiastic feasts. After inducing vomiting, they would return to the feast and start all over again. "Ah-ha," we thought, "here's a way to not have our cake and eat it, too!" We could indulge our compulsions without having to face the consequences of getting fat. . . . I had absolutely no idea that I was establishing an indulgence/deprivation cycle that would become psychologically and physically addictive. The more we vomited ourselves into emptiness, the more we needed to eat.*

Jane Fonda continued purging for several years after high school. While in college, she was put on weight reducing drugs that were then popular but are now known to be dangerous and also physically addictive. As a young, successful actress in Hollywood, she continued to use these drugs and to purge until she consulted a holistic doctor in

London and learned about the serious health problems these practices cause. Now, she relies on exercise and a healthful diet to keep herself in shape and feeling good.

## THE MEDICAL CONSEQUENCES

Many bulimics binge on primarily starchy and sugary foods. Since they often consume mammoth quantities of these foods, their teeth are especially vulnerable to excessive decay. Those bulimics who vomit risk stripping their tooth enamel and, from using fingers or devices to induce regurgitation, damaging the teeth and lining of the mouth.

The vomiting bulimic also can injure the linings of the esophagus and stomach. In rare cases, vomiting has caused the esophagus to rupture, and this has sometimes proven fatal.

Often, the female bulimic stops menstruating when the disorder becomes serious. This is a warning that the body is not getting the nutrition it needs, and therefore it automatically shuts off one of its complex and important functions. The loss of menstrual periods is called *amenorrhea*. It can occur also in women who are active in sports, and for a variety of other physical and psychological reasons. Many bulimics never lose their periods; others have irregular cycles. When a certain amount of weight is lost, the woman usually stops menstruating. For this reason, amenorrhea is often an early sign of anorexia. When periods become irregular or cease, a psychiatrist, internist, pediatrician, or gynecologist specially trained in eating disorders should be contacted.

The use of laxatives and diuretics, medicines which eliminate solid and liquid wastes from the body, seems, at first, to offer many bulimics an alternative to vomiting. But, in order to rid their bodies of large amounts of food in a short period of time, bulimics must seriously abuse these medications. When binging and purging on a continual basis, the bulimic may take up to several hundred doses of these medications a week. Vital liquids and minerals are eliminated from the body. This causes dehydration, muscle cramps, and dizziness. The body begins to depend on laxatives if they are used on a regular basis, and the bowels can no longer be moved without them.

Sodium, potassium, and magnesium are three vital conducting elements (electrolytes) in the body's "electrical" system. This electrical system, which requires a balance of electrolytes, is needed for various bodily functions such as digestion. Vomiting and the use of medicines to purge causes these vital elements to be lost. At first, this causes fatigue, cramps, and sometimes dizziness and fainting. When purging continues on an intensive basis, it can cause kidney damage and, eventually kidney and heart failure. Bulimics and anorectics who binge and purge have died from the heart failure that an electrolyte imbalance can cause. When stopped early, with the help of a physician, this damage can often be reversed as the electrolyte balance is restored.

## FASTING

As we have seen, some bulimics punish themselves for binging by resorting to fasting. This method has many of the health hazards of other purging methods, as well as the additional danger of damaging the liver. When someone begins to fast, the body goes into an emergency state. Since it can't get the blood sugar (glucose) usually taken from food to feed the brain and other organs, it calls upon the small amount of glucose stored in the liver. This is depleted by the end of the first day. After that, the body must provide for its needs by breaking down the proteins found in organs and muscle tissue. The body finally uses fatty deposits only after several days, to protect the heart and other muscles from destruction. Even then, fat is broken down incompletely. These are only some of the known dangers of fasting; others may still be undiscovered.

Teenagers especially need protein because their bodies are still developing, so fasting is more dangerous for them than it is for adults. Also, most fasters suffer from rebounds—many of them gain considerable weight after they resume eating, and become heavier than they were originally. Their bodies try both to make up for what they have lost and to store fat in case of future fasts.

## FASTING BUDDHISTS
## AND SUFFRAGETTES

In her book, *Eating Disorders,* Dr. Hilde Bruch reviews the long history of fasting. In the ancient Far East, a person could "fast against" someone for revenge, even to the point of sitting on the enemy's doorstep and making an embarrassing public display. Fasting for religious purposes also has been a tradition, especially in the East where priests and disciples follow Buddha's example by seeking the path to enlightenment by denying themselves food.

When India was fighting for its independence from England, Gandhi, a world renowned pacifist and Hindu nationalist, fasted to call attention to his country's political struggles. In England, suffragettes, women seeking the right to vote, went on hunger strikes when they were jailed. In 1982, women in the United States fasted to seek passage of the Equal Rights Amendment. The hunger strike has also been a vehicle to publicize the political situations of labor groups, prisoners, and social reformers. Those who refuse to eat attract a certain amount of admiration and curiosity. Although political fasts often do gain public attention, they don't always bring about the desired changes. Unless there is an opponent sensitive enough to be swayed by the person's or group's fast, it is a wasted effort.

Dr. Bruch quotes from Eric Erikson's book, *Gandhi's Truth,* to explain the paradox implicit in political fasting:

> *It should be clear that there cannot really be any "pure" decision to starve one's self to death, for such determination can only emerge from a paradoxical combination of a passionate belief in the absolute vitality of certain living issues and the determination to die for them: thus one "lives up" to a principle by dying for it.*

With such a colorful history, fasting appeals to some bulimics as a viable alternate to both uncontrollable eating and the distasteful practice of purging. They may even imagine themselves to be political heroes, or feel a sense of superiority because they can control their hunger and deny their need for food.

## SANDY'S PERFECT WEIGHT

At sixteen, Sandy tried out for the cheerleading squad. She worked hard to learn the cheers, but deep down she knew she didn't have a chance. Although her mother said she was "cute" and at a good weight, she knew she was fat. At 125 pounds (56 kg), she felt as if she were surrounded by a gross layer of fat that shook when she did handstands and clapped out cheers. She didn't make the cheerleading squad just as she hadn't gotten dates or the very best grades. Joking with her friends wasn't enough to soothe the disappointment. Neither was eating her favorite junk foods.

Sandy decided to go on a diet to get down to the perfect weight of 110 pounds (50 kg). She knew it would make a big difference in her life. She knew food and fat were the "enemies" ruining her chances for success.

First, she tried a high protein diet from a magazine. It didn't work fast enough, so she cut back on her food a little more, weighing every morsel and calculating the calories before she ate anything. She hated dieting and longed for her favorite snacks. But instead of heading for the refrigerator, she forced herself to keep drinking diet soda and coffee.

She achieved her desired weight in three weeks. Suddenly, she was "New York model" thin, with gentle curves. Her friends marvelled at the change in her. She was proud of her self-discipline and success. Boys noticed her more, and she started dating Evan, a popular student from the debating team. She felt perfect, at a magic weight that promised a magic life.

When she didn't make the debating team, the old fears came back. Was she really still too fat? Why wasn't the magic weight working? She went back to eating junk food, not in limited quantities, as she had before, but frantically buying and eating more than she ever had.

Putting the food in her mouth felt good. But after it reached her stomach, panic set in. She would be fat again, a nobody, because of that dreaded layer around her body. She imagined her new image fading and Evan losing interest. She borrowed her mother's laxative. She had to get the enemy, food, out of her body before it ruined her life.

When her mother got suspicious, Sandy switched to

vomiting. It was difficult at first, and then it felt soothing and relaxing. She had discovered the secret to staying at a perfect weight while still enjoying her favorite foods. Once again, she felt magical, possessed of a secret power, a new weapon to fight fat.

Ten years later, Sandy was still drinking diet soda and black coffee between binging on junk food and purging. She was still at that magic, perfect weight of 110 pounds (50 kg). She had worked hard and risen from secretary to junior executive in the large corporation for which she worked. Everyone was impressed with her ''business flair,'' and she believed this meant her perfect appearance. Her job included traveling to meet with people all over the country. She had to be aggressive, but not too pushy, a balance she found difficult to achieve.

When she stopped seeing the lawyer whom she had been dating for a year, the strain was too much. She revealed to her mother her decade-long history of binging and purging. Her mother, who had been suspicious for years, was nevertheless shocked.

Sandy realized that her perfect weight had not brought her total success. Like many other bulimics, she had had to hide her purging and, eventually, had felt isolated instead of special. With counseling and medical help, Sandy is now changing her long habit of food abuse. She has switched to a job she likes even better than her old one, and is dating a new man. She still has to keep convincing herself that it's all right to weigh more than 110 pounds (50 kg).

Eileen, Jane Fonda, and Sandy are just a few of the thousands of women who have been afflicted with the hidden disease of bulimia. Although each story is different, for all those involved it is a difficult road back to normal attitudes and habits concerning eating and weight.

# FIVE

## BULIMIA:
## CAUSES AND CURES

As is the case with other eating disorders, there is no single cause of bulimia. It has been a known phenomenon only for the past few years, and many clues to its origins are still emerging. There is an obvious contributing factor: TV advertising invites viewers to overindulge in tempting food, and then tells them they had better watch their weight and drink diet cola. We are all confused by these inconsistent messages, and it's easy to see how they would particularly confuse someone with bulimic tendencies.

Many of the other causes of bulimia are less easy to see. There are complex emotional factors and personal experiences that include family attitudes, pressures to succeed, unfulfilled desires and dreams, and peer group pressures, which can cause some susceptible people to become bulimic.

### NO CLEAR PHYSICAL CAUSE
If bulimia were caused by a bodily malfunction, a medicine could probably be formulated to cure it. Unfortunately, no physical causes have been discovered. Rarely, someone with a brain tumor or other physical ailment will be mistaken

for a bulimic because of his or her irregular appetite and frequent regurgitation. One big difference is that a bulimic willingly induces purging. Unlike many bulimics, a person with a physically induced eating disorder will usually openly seek help, and will do it sooner. Even though the bulimic chooses to release stress by binging and purging, she will often say she has no control over her food binges, and may even say, "The food just comes up on its own." This is possible only after purging has become a habit.

It is often easier for the bulimic to imagine a physical cause for her problems than to deal with the complex emotional factors behind them. A pamphlet from the Center for the Study of Anorexia and Bulimia in New York clearly states the range of causes of bulimia: "Experts are in agreement that bulimia is *not* the result of a physical condition, and that it is *not* a disorder that can occur in just about anybody. Bulimia is an emotional disorder that gets its start and becomes entrenched as a result of specific psychological conflicts."

## THAT EMPTY FEELING
Bulimics often speak of a deep, emotional "hunger" that seizes them suddenly. Like a compulsive eater, the bulimic hopes that, by stuffing her mouth and stomach full of food, she will feel better and lose that empty feeling inside. Often, she has problems too overwhelming to face or too deep-rooted to be recognized easily. Food, to the bulimic, means comfort, a refuge. It brings that full, rich feeling we have all experienced when we sit down to a hot, home-cooked meal with family or friends.

But the bulimic consumes much more than she can comfortably hold, usually thousands to tens of thousands of calories of starch and sugary junk foods in one sitting. Instead of helping, the food binge generates guilt and more

# THE SPIRALING EFFECTS
# OF BINGING AND PURGING

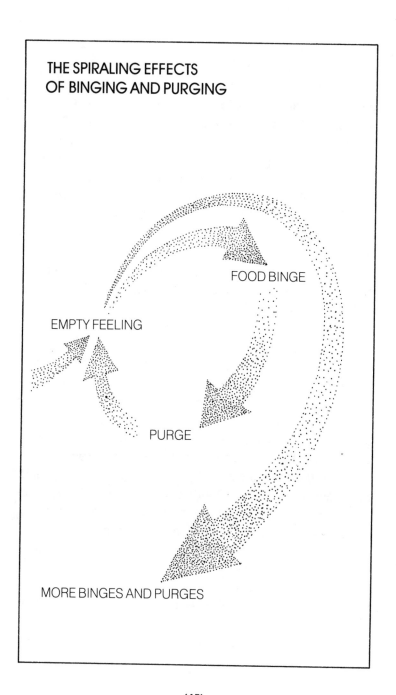

FOOD BINGE

EMPTY FEELING

PURGE

MORE BINGES AND PURGES

frustration. Her stomach becomes overfilled and uncomfortable; she panics and purges her stomach of food.

Purging has been described by bulimics as "a high, pure feeling, almost religious." The relief the bulimic feels is temporary, though, and she pays a high price for it. Purging practices themselves cause throat, esophagus, and stomach lining damages and/or dependence on medications. Little of the vast amount of food is properly digested and, after its swift removal, the bulimic faces an increased hunger and even stronger feeling of emptiness.

## FAMILY ROOTS

Many therapists see the family's role in the development of eating disorders as a crucial and primary one. In the case of bulimia, early studies showed that a large majority of women involved were high school and college students from middle-class and upper-middle-class backgrounds, where success was stressed and expected. Although it is now known that there are bulimics from all kinds of backgrounds, this family history is commonly seen.

Bulimics often have successful parents and ambitious brothers and sisters. They are taught early that they are expected to be the best in whatever they do. Some mothers of bulimics are unsure of how to treat their children, and this may cause their daughters to lack self-esteem. The daughter feels that, no matter how hard she tries, she will not do well enough to win her mother's approval.

Fathers of bulimics tend to be distant, preoccupied with work, but nevertheless they expect their daughters to get first-rate grades and to be "picture perfect." Some may have difficulty really listening to or talking with their daughters. A bulimic may see her father as a potential source of great strength, but feel that his strength is not available to her. She may feel that no matter how hard she tries, she will not really be able to please him.

In some cases, a family's attitude about food is an important factor. Snacking may be a family habit, or the family may be very strict about allowing desserts and junk food. One or more family members may constantly diet because of a real or imagined weight problem. In many families of bulimics, physical appearance is as important as success. Family members are encouraged to strive for material, tangible goals like good grades, honors, high status jobs, and the "right" social connections, while keeping physically fit and as attractive as possible. The family of a bulimic may look like the perfect American family. But the tension, emotional distance, and frustration within the family may overwhelm the bulimic. She sees herself as unable to be a worthwhile, productive part of this "wonderful" family. She feels something important is missing, something that perhaps she can find in food. But, after binging, she fears the consequences. She knows she must purge to avoid weight gain, to get rid of the evidence that she has been out of control, an imperfect daughter.

Sometimes, the mother of a bulimic is frustrated about her own life or career. Perhaps she has had to quit a high-paying job or interrupt her professional training to raise her children. Perhaps she has been forced to take a less fulfilling part-time job so she will have time for her family. The repressed rage and frustration she may feel can cause her to pressure her daughter to achieve the success she never had. In earlier times in Hollywood, women who pushed their children into show business were called "stage-mothers." Many fathers, uncles, aunts, brothers, and sisters also try to live out their unfulfilled dreams and desires through their close relatives. This kind of pressure can trigger bulimia.

A mother and her bulimic daughter may be confused about their roles as women. They may seem highly-motivated and successful, while they may be repressing needs to be loved and sheltered. When these needs are unrecognized or unfulfilled, problems arise.

Dr. John Sours, in his book *Starving to Death in a Sea of Objects*, recalls a sixteen-year-old anorectic patient whose bulimic behavior was closely linked to family origins:

> *In consultation, Joanne stated that she 'hated school, hard work, ambition, and her father's attitude of no fun.' Speaking of these things seemed to make her stomach jerk in as though she would vomit the statement. Compulsively ambitious and monomaniacal about rising above his immigrant background, her father worked eighteen hours a day in his small business and insisted his children work for at least Ph.D.'s.*

Joanne was jealous of an older brother, whom she felt received more of the family's attention. She also claimed that her mother was "selfishly overprotective," yet not really caring or understanding. Joanne's anger and rage at her family were expressed in her pattern of binging and purging. In her case, she also lost weight, going from 125 pounds (56 kg) down to 95 pounds (43 kg). Although she was diagnosed as anorectic because of her weight loss, her binging and purging were principal parts of her disorder.

## DISTORTED BODY IMAGE
Dr. Hilde Bruch uses the term "distorted body image" to describe the confusion many people with eating disorders

feel when viewing their image in the mirror or comparing their size to that of others. These people have a self-image different from reality, as if a carnival mirror were distorting their physical appearance.

Bulimics often feel they are too fat, even though their weight falls 10 to 15 pounds (5 to 7 kg) below the average weight for their age and height. Or they feel they are grossly overweight when they have an extra pound or two. Instead of maintaining the weight that is normal for them, bulimics try to achieve the undernourished figures of models.

The distorted body image of the bulimic is due in part to our society's equation of thin with beautiful. Although recent studies have shown that a person with up to 10 to 15 percent of extra weight is healthier and less prone to disease than someone 10 to 15 percent underweight, we regard underweight models as beautiful. The bulimic's normal size that would result from a healthful diet and from her inherited body characteristics often is larger than this skinny build.

## A NEAR-STARVATION DIET

Most bulimics claim that their problems got out of hand after strict dieting. The pressure from these regimes caused them to binge for relief, and then to purge. Losing a little weight does not bring the dieter the dreamed-of happiness, nor does it solve her problems. Stress from dieting and disappointment after the initial weight has been lost create new problems.

Dr. Bruch refers to these unhappy people who have lost weight, yet still have their original problems, as "thin fat people." Although they now have the "perfect" appearance they have sought, it hasn't helped them to feel better about themselves. In fact, some people still have a distorted body image after they have attained their desired weight.

The actual dieting process—skipping meals and eating only meager portions—creates its own problems. Dr. Bruch names some of them: "tension, bad disposition, irritability and inability to pursue an educational or professional goal."

In some cases, the diet backfires, causing more problems than the dieter ever dreamed possible.

## HELP FOR BULIMICS

Because of the public outcry about bulimia during the past few years, there are now many treatment options. Bulimics can find help in their own communities or on their college campuses through both traditional and innovative therapies, self-help groups, and experienced medical doctors. There are also support and research groups around the country. Therapy ranges from traditional one-to-one exploration of the bulimic's deep emotional problems to hypnotherapy and family systems analysis. It may also take the form of behavior modification programs designed to alter or replace eating rituals with more constructive alternatives.

Since there are so many different treatment programs available, the bulimic has a good chance of finding one that works specifically for her. There are two important factors to consider when choosing a treatment program: (1) the therapists or group leaders should be experienced in dealing with eating disorders, and (2) the bulimic should feel comfortable with and trusting of therapists or other group members. This trust may take a few meetings or sessions to develop, but it is important for recovery. If the bulimic seeking treatment is made to feel like a strange, unique patient with a rare disorder, this may be a clue that a more sophisticated treatment facility is needed.

## A MUST FOR BULIMICS

Because binging and purging can lead to severe bodily damage and in extreme cases, death, the bulimic needs a thorough evaluation from a competent internist, a medical doctor specializing in the internal functioning of the body. The bulimic should be completely frank about the nature and duration of the purging practices she has engaged in. This will enable the doctor to work toward reversing any physical damage that has been done. Sometimes, in short-term cases, there is little irreversible damage. Sadly, though, there are many cases of recovering bulimics who thought that treatment of their emotional problems was enough, and have died from the cumulative physiological effects of their binging and purging over long periods of time.

## THE FIRST STEP

Reaching out for help is the most difficult step a bulimic can take, but also the most important. By asking for help, she is admitting that her problem is out of control. This is especially difficult for someone who is considered successful by others and whose goals do not leave room for any failures.

## ONE-TO-ONE THERAPY

Traditional psychotherapy, as well as other one-to-one therapies, are carried out through individual sessions with a psychiatrist, psychologist, or psychiatric social worker specially trained to give counseling. The more traditional methods include an exploration of the bulimic's feelings, experiences, family, and childhood in order to find out the deep-rooted causes of his or her behavior. This usually involves the interpretation of dreams, actions, and desires. The therapist may use hypnosis, meditation, or other techniques to help the bulimic to explore herself. This deep exploration takes anywhere from a few months to several years. Some therapists feel that it is really the only way to get the bulimic to deal with her problems and become completely cured.

Since bulimia is an emotional disorder with possible serious physical complications, traditional one-to-one therapy is sometimes too slow to prevent or stop damage to the bulimic's body. Sometimes, it is combined with or replaced by other methods that bring a quicker end to the bulimic's binging and purging. Behavior modification is one technique often used to achieve speedy recovery. It involves changing current behavior patterns rather than looking at the reasons behind them. This is usually done by rewarding improved behavior and withdrawing privileges or punishing the patient for negative behavior. The bulimic agrees to a specific system of rewards and punishments and may actually sign a "contract."

She is then taught how to substitute healthier practices for her bulimic rituals. She is also shown how to deal with the panic she feels when she has a full stomach. The specific lessons and experiences gradually help the bulimic to unlearn her self-destructive behavior.

Behavior modification was once regarded as a miracle cure for eating disorders because of its capacity to stop swiftly the gorging of compulsive eaters and the near-fasting of anorectics. However, many bulimics find this approach cold and clinical. Some rebel against it. Others return to binging and purging after their contracts are up. Long-term studies have shown that behavior modification usually does not insure a long-lasting cure. Often, behavior modification is used to alleviate immediate, serious health problems, while some other forms of therapy explore the underlying causes of the bulimic's disorder.

## GROUP THERAPY

A bulimic may react to her first group therapy meeting by saying, "I'm not alone. My secret is not so terrible after all."

This sense of relief can launch a bulimic on the road to recovery. She hears others with the same problem talking about their panic, fear, triumphs, failures, and daily struggles. In a group of recovering bulimics, there is much support and sharing. Feelings of isolation and guilt can be changed to a new, healthy outlook. When one bulimic finds a way to overcome her destructive patterns, she can serve as an example and inspiration to others. The cure can be contagious.

Some groups are led by recovering bulimics who want both support and the chance to help others. Others are conducted by psychotherapists and college counselors. Groups are also available for the families and friends of those suffering from bulimia and other eating disorders. Many groups are established by grass-roots organizations such as the American Anorexia Nervosa Association, and research centers such as the Center for the Study of Anorexia and Bulimia. Research facilities are located in several major cities and at many universities. Organizations like Overeaters Anonymous have recently started sponsoring some groups for bulimics, too. To find out about group therapy in a specific community, consult the psychotherapy listing in the phone book, check the newspapers, or write to one of the information centers listed at the back of this book.

Although nearly all experts agree that group interaction is an important element in the recovery of many bulimics, some feel it should be supplemented by individual therapy because one person's problems cannot always be considered in depth in a group setting. All experts agree that group therapy is *never* a substitute for a complete physical examination with a competent internist.

**FAMILY THERAPY**

Since many therapists and experts see the family's role as primary in the development of bulimia, they also recognize the importance of treating the entire family rather than just the bulimic individual. Family therapists reason that if the bulimic is treated individually, but her family's problems and negative influences remain the same, there is no possibility of a meaningful cure.

The entire family participates in sessions, along with the bulimic. Family members explore their patterns of interaction with the bulimic and are encouraged to see how their attitudes and behavior affect the bulimic. No one is ever blamed for causing the bulimia. In fact, many family members find relief from the guilt and frustration caused by the bulimic's distressing practices. Some family members are encouraged to seek additional help. Sometimes, the parents of a bulimic seek marital counseling. Often, after therapy, the family attempts to communicate more with one another, and to change its attitudes toward the bulimic relative.

Proponents of family therapy claim that it is really the *only* way to get to the roots of the problem swiftly, and to change the bulimic's destructive patterns. Critics, many of them therapists who use other techniques, claim that family therapy is more useful as a complement to individual therapy. They point out that often key family members are unwilling to undergo therapy. Sometimes, too, the family unit is too fragile to benefit from it. Although there is disagreement as to the value of family therapy for helping bulimics in every case, most therapists agree that, in many instances, it is highly valuable.

# SIX

---

# ANOREXIA NERVOSA: STARVING YOURSELF TO DEATH

The photos of the teenage girl show only a skeleton, just skin and bones. Her rib, hip, and knee bones protrude. Her stomach is bloated and resembles a small basketball. She looks like a concentration camp victim, but she isn't. Although she had been starved she had done it to herself while surrounded by food. She is a victim of the eating disorder known as anorexia nervosa.

Anorexia nervosa is considered the most serious of eating disorders because 10 to 15 percent of its victims die. The families and friends of anorectics watch them change from active, healthy young women to morbid, hostile phantoms as the disease takes over. But the anorectic perceives her skeleton-like appearance as an indication of her power to defy her need for food. This ability to ignore the seriousness of her emaciated condition frightens her family and friends. As one roommate of an anorectic said, "I was afraid that if I said the wrong thing, she would die."

Anorexia was once a rare disease affecting only a few people, many of them wealthy. In the past twenty years, it has been occurring more often, particularly in junior high and high schools. Recent statistics indicate that as many as one in every one hundred students between sixteen and eighteen years of age develops anorexia. College and high school officials in the United States are alarmed at the growing number of coeds stricken by the disease. Up to 3,750 deaths a year have been attributed to anorexia nervosa. Although far fewer women suffer from anorexia than bulimia, anorexia has attracted more attention from medical doctors, writers, and the public because its effects are so visible and horrifying.

The famous singing star, Karen Carpenter, who recently died from cardiac arrest, was said to have been suffering from anorexia nervosa. Doctors agreed that the disorder could have damaged the singer's heart.

A poem by Laura R. Bronstein, which first appeared in the literary journal *Tightrope 9,* portrays the rage that many anorectics feel toward others, but direct back upon themselves:

                    animus anorexia

                    passing
                    the meat and
                    potatoes
                    by
                    as if
                    by
                    starv
                    ing
                    her
                    self
                    she
                    cld
                    kll
                    hm

## WHAT IT MEANS

*Anorexia nervosa* literally means a lack of hunger due to nerves. It was misnamed long ago when doctors believed that it was caused by extreme nervousness or by stomach problems. Now, it is known that anorectics do feel hunger. In fact, they feel very intense hunger as they starve their bodies willingly. While they deprive themselves of nutrients, they dream constantly of food and often tempt others to overeat. Many anorectics claim they can feel full just by watching others eat. Their hunger sometimes drives them to binge and purge or to consume only certain favorite foods in strange, ritualistic ways.

The words "anorexia nervosa" helped to foster confusion about the disease itself. Until recently, anyone who refused to eat because of a psychological problem or a physical ailment might have been diagnosed as anorectic. In the past few years, researchers like Dr. Hilde Bruch have helped to distinguish the disease from other disorders. They have identified a specific group of behavior patterns that are linked with certain emotional and physical characteristics.

According to Dr. Bruch, many mental patients suffering from other problems exhibit anorectic tendencies during their illnesses and treatments. She distinguishes these patients from those suffering from anorexia primarily by calling them "atypical anorectics." Those completely caught up in anorexia and following its distinctive patterns of behavior and attitudes are called "primary anorectics."

It is sometimes difficult to distinguish between primary and atypical anorexia because starvation of any kind brings on abnormal mental characteristics. The body is deprived of its needed energy, so the brain does not function in its usual way. People fasting for political reasons or starving in prison camps have developed some of the same delusions and mental problems as advanced anorectics.

## THE BASIC FACTS

Anorexia nervosa is now recognized as a distinct set of behavioral patterns and attitudes centered around the anorectic's desire to avoid food and keep her body at an abnormal weight, usually 25 percent lower than is considered normal for her age and height. Ninety percent of the known victims of anorexia are female. Most of them are between eleven and twenty years old. Many start their starvation with a very rigid diet, and then become obsessed with their ability to lose weight easily. They come to actually fear food and the possibility of gaining weight.

Anorectics are intensely proud of their thinness, even when it upsets others. As one anorectic said, "I was convinced that I could be the skinniest ever and no one was going to stop me."

Many anorectics come from wealthy or comfortable middle-class homes where food and material possessions are readily available. Most are termed "sweet, hard-working, and well-behaved" before the disease takes over. Only a few come from broken homes. Although many anorectics describe their families as "wonderful," there are often hidden tensions, power struggles, and deep-seated confusion among the family members. Often, someone else in the family has had a physical or emotional ailment. Sometimes, the anorectic has tried to be perfect for years to please her family or to compensate for something lacking in her home life. This "perfect" facade breaks down when she becomes a teenager.

## MALE ANORECTICS

According to most reports, at least 90 percent of all known anorectics are female. But some therapists and researchers feel that male anorectics are not always recognized as such. Dr. John Sours, in his book, *Starving to Death in a Sea of Objects,* summarizes the findings of four prominent researchers who found that anorexia in males was often misdiagnosed because doctors did not expect to find male anorectics. He points out that two of the earliest documented cases of anorexia were a starving buddha in the third century A.D. and a Persian prince in the eleventh century.

Dr. Sours has found that male anorectics have many of the same symptoms as female ones. "Usually their disturbance begins in prepuberty; dauntless dieters, they are fearful of fatness, femininity, and sexuality."

## LINK WITH
## COMPULSIVE EATING

Anorexia has been called the opposite extreme of compulsive eating. But it really can't be described that simply because many compulsive eaters vary their binges with periods of fasting. Anorectics also have periods of intense eating. Some become compulsive eaters after they're "cured" of anorexia, or have a history of compulsive eating before they begin their starvation diets. In both disorders food is obviously a problem, but the underlying causes are complex emotional ones. Anorexia and compulsive eating should be thought of as two different aberrations in which food is used to indicate that something is wrong psychologically. Because many of the reasons behind each are similar, many of the same therapies and cures are used to treat both disorders.

## LINK WITH BULIMIA

Many anorectics either binge on food or consider eating any small amount of it a binge. Then they purge by using laxatives, diuretics, self-induced vomiting, or fasting. They are even more concerned than bulimics that food not stay in their small stomachs. The physical problems associated with bulimia, such as dehydration, damage to the organs, and chemical imbalances are often more severe when they occur in an anorectic who is already starving herself.

Recent research shows a significant percentage of bulimics with a history of anorexia. Some studies have found that as many as half of the known anorectics engage in bulimic practices during or after their anorectic period. In extreme cases, some recovering anorectics who practiced binging and purging have died due to the cumulative effects of both eating disorders.

## EILEEN AT SEVENTEEN

Eileen is now nearly thirty, the mother of a young child, a bright, inventive, charming woman. She is still haunted, though, by the combination of anorexia and bulimia, which began with a strict diet when she was seventeen.

Here is her story:

*When I was about seventeen, I started changing from a girl to a woman. At that age, your body starts changing. You have hips and breasts. I was having trouble dealing with not being the "stick" I used to be.*

*I probably gained about 7 or 8 pounds, from 115 to 123. I thought I was huge. So, I hardly ever ate anything. I'd get up in the morning and I wouldn't eat. I'd get on my bicycle and ride for miles. My stomach would burn and I'd get lightheaded. I'd feel like my body was caving in on itself.*

*I never got really skinny. I know that my hipbones stuck way out and you could see my rib bones. I worked at the library and the counter was about the height of my hips and I'd get huge bruises because I had no padding.*

*You'd love to feel hungry. You'd love to feel that you were starving yourself because that was what it was all about. The more you starved yourself, the less you ate, the skinnier you got. You just loved it and you wanted more, so you could go for days without eating. I remember, especially when I was riding my bicycle, I would feel dizzy and that would make me feel high because I knew I was pushing myself—pushing, pushing, pushing and exercising and burning off all those calories.*

Eileen did not starve to death. As with some anorectics, her weight leveled off before it reached a critical point. She continued to have periods of intense fasting when she entered college and became bulimic. She never got help for her eating disorders because it wasn't readily available at that time. Her anorectic tendencies were moderate compared to the horror stories of many other teenagers.

## THE BEST LITTLE GIRL
In his fictional book, *The Best Little Girl in the World,* Steven Levenkron, a well-known therapist who has developed a workable method for dealing with anorexia, chronicles the descent into the disease and its complications. The heroine, Francesca, is a composite, representative of

many of the patients Levenkron has treated. Francesca's problems become apparent during a dance class as she starts to feel obsessively concerned about her weight and her ability to be the best dancer. She changes her name from Francesca to Kessa, and chants her new name and counts obsessively during meals to keep from eating. Kessa tears out from magazines photos of models, and ranks each for thinness. She throws away the corresponding picture as she becomes gradually thinner and begins to reach her goal of extreme weight loss. Her motto becomes, "The thinner is the winner."

The less she eats, the stranger her rituals become. She does not allow her fork to touch her lips as she eats.

When she has lost a noticeable amount of weight, her parents grow concerned. But she has already sunk deep into her "magic" rituals and steadily loses more weight.

After she has been to two internists and a psychiatrist, she is still losing weight. Just as she begins to trust another therapist, her weight loss becomes critical. She has lost over a third of her body's weight and is a walking skeleton.

Entering the hospital creates new problems. She feels betrayed by her family and therapist. The night before she is to be linked to a feeding tube, she panics:

> She ran her hands over her body as if to bid it good-bye. The hipbones rising from a shrunken stomach were razor-sharp. Would they be lost in a sea of fat? She counted her ribs, bone by bone. Where would they go? She squeezed one arm and then the other. Would they blow up like great puffed sleeves of flesh? She pressed against her stomach till the pain was excruciating. There was

*so little time before they put the tube in. If only she could lose a few more pounds.*

She tries to walk, but instead collapses. She is close to death as the doctors and nurses work frantically to save her life. After she has had the tube attached, her physical health improves very slowly, but her mental traumas persist. With the help of her therapist, roommate, and sessions with her family, she begins to realize some of the issues behind her starvation.

One breakthrough occurs when the therapist points out some of the fears behind her rituals. He speaks to her as if he were thinking aloud for her: ". . . if I cut up my food a certain way or only eat certain things or don't eat certain things, I might protect myself from other people's bad feelings. . . ."

Finally, Kessa begins to see how her eating habits have taken over her life. And her family begins to realize that they must love and support her for being good, not just when she does something as desperate as starving herself. There is no immediate happy ending, but there are many important steps toward recovery.

Public awareness of anorexia as a life-threatening disease has increased greatly over the past twenty years. Although Eileen never got help for her problems, Kessa was eventually able to find treatment even though her parents' initial attempts were not successful. There are many clear warning signs that can alert the family, friends, and the anorectic herself that she is endangering her health.

## PULLING AWAY

One of the earliest signs of anorexia is a pulling away from loved ones and friends. The experts say that this may occur as early as a year or more before the anorectic has stopped eating. It intensifies as she becomes involved with and secretive about her food rituals. Many anorectics, previously regarded as ideal students and loving family members, suddenly become rude and uncommunicative. Or, the change may come very slowly, sometimes too slowly for family members and friends to notice.

As she withdraws from most activities and people, the anorectic may devote her energy to one activity or to thinking about one idol. At first, her behavior appears to be the normal hero worship commonly engaged in by teenagers. But soon it develops into an obsession, and people around her realize something is wrong.

Anorexia is one of the loneliest diseases. Unlike a patient with a physically-caused ailment, the anorectic herself has willingly caused her illness. Many family members and friends react to her condition with guilt, anger, and even rage. Because the anorectic defies the normal eating patterns of those around her and often horrifies others, she must pull away from those she has cared about in order to keep starving herself. As the disease develops, the initial distance she has felt becomes greatly intensified.

## LOSS OF MENSTRUAL PERIOD
Often, one of the earliest signs that the anorectic's body is not getting enough food is the loss of her menstrual periods. The medical term for loss of periods is *amenorrhea*. In the case of anorectics who have not yet started menstruating, it may mean the delay of onset for several months or years. Some teenage anorectics have never had a period, and some with recurring cases enter their twenties without ever having menstruated. When it doesn't get the nutrition it needs, the body begins to cease performing certain functions. Since menstruation is needed in order to bear children, a starving woman ceases to menstruate because

she could not easily bear a healthy child. When an anorectic goes without periods for a long time, she risks becoming permanently unable to bear children.

## RESTLESS ENERGY

Another early warning sign of anorexia is a continuous restless energy, which is called *hyperactivity*. Although the anorectic is not getting enough to eat, she keeps going as though her body were well-fueled. She knows that she will burn up calories by staying constantly in motion, and the activity also helps to keep her mind off the physical pain of starvation.

Eileen rode her bike without eating. Kessa, determined to be the best ballet dancer in the world, exercised her starving body even when she was exhausted. Many anorectics are obsessed with jogging or other sports. Some constantly pace and keep moving. An anorectic may tell herself that she is going to walk fifteen extra blocks one day. The next day it's a required part of her daily schedule, and soon she is again increasing the number of blocks.

Some anorectics use their restless energy in order to study or work late into the night. By focusing on school work or the demands of their jobs, they can take their minds off fears that often plague them late at night.

As the anorectic's condition gets worse, she may lose interest in the sports or activities she was obsessed with before. She no longer has the energy to keep moving, but she may keep up her activity longer than it would have been thought possible. As she exercises her unpadded bones, she may suffer from injuries and sustain bruises.

When anorexia is highly advanced, its victim will no longer be able to keep moving vigorously, although she may still be hyperactive. She may suffer discomfort from any movement at all, and will spend more and more time sleeping.

## DISTORTED BODY IMAGE

The anorectic sees her emaciated body as fat, and is not aware that she is near death. She knows that everyone else thinks she is too thin, but she agonizes over every minor bulge or over any part of her body that is not completely skeletal. This distorted body image becomes more deeply ingrained as the disease progresses.

One of the tools some therapists use is a mirror, but it isn't enough for the anorectic to view her skeleton body. She must be taught to view her body as it actually is, an important, but painstaking, process.

## FOOD GAMES

At various stages of anorexia, its victim will play strange games with food. She may divide a cookie into twenty small pieces, then take hours to eat them all. Like Kessa, she may decide the food cannot touch her lips. She may lure her friends into an ice cream store, talking about all the flavors and toppings, then get a diet sherbert and throw most of it away. Because food both intrigues and frightens anorectics, the sight and smell of certain foods as they are cooking can cause extreme reactions.

Some anorectics hide food even after it is rotten. They may eat food not realizing that it has gone bad. They become so obsessed by their rituals that they don't really taste the food that they do allow themselves to eat.

When anorectics lose control and binge, or just feel the discomfort that having food inside their shrunken stomachs causes, they often purge. Many leave the family dinner table after having been forced to eat or after having

**(67)**

chosen to eat just a minuscule amount. They want to rid themselves of the food as fast as possible.

Some anorectics cook rich gourmet foods for their families and friends. They rejoice when others put on weight. Their abstinence is more meaningful when others eat without restraint. They project their hunger onto others as if they can get rid of it that way.

## SENSITIVITY TO COLD

Since the anorectic's body is not getting the fuel it needs and doesn't have any fat left to protect it, she is often cold even in the summer. Anorectics may wear layers of clothes to insulate themselves, or brave the cold in defiance of the fact that their shrunken bodies cannot tolerate it.

One mechanism that the body has, when highly depleted and unable to keep warm, is to grow a fine layer of downy hair, called *lanugo,* over its surface. This allows the body to retain more heat and protect itself from the cold. Anorectics often develop this layer of lanugo as their illness advances.

## OTHER SIGNS

There are many other signs that someone is anorectic. The most obvious one is that they have lost considerable weight, usually about 25 percent of their normal size. Although this weight loss may be gradual, those living with or near the anorectic can usually notice it. A loss of head hair, pale and discolored skin, and a generally unhealthy look is usually apparent as the disease gets serious.

The sufferer's mental condition deteriorates as the disease gets worse. The anorectic may suffer from loss of memory, outbursts of temper, the inability to concentrate, and various phobias, obsessions, and psychoses.

## GETTING HELP

Anyone suffering from several of the warning signs listed above may have anorexia or some other physically-caused disease. Sufferers will need medical help to determine the nature of their problem, and the support of those around them. The families and friends of anorectics often feel both guilty and horrified when anorexia develops. Most communities now have professionals experienced in the treatment of anorexia and other eating disorders, who can help both the patient and her family and friends deal with the dilemmas of the disease.

It is important to seek professional aid as early as possible. Most experts agree that the sooner an anorectic gets help, the better are her chances of recovery, both physically and mentally. It is also crucial to find the best professional help available; if possible, someone experienced in treating anorectic patients. Because an anorectic's health may be in immediate danger, and her mental condition is especially difficult to treat, special techniques have been developed. There is a listing of several national and regional information, treatment, and referral organizations at the back of this book. These groups are often able to direct sufferers and those wishing to help them to the nearest experienced professionals.

# SEVEN

## ANOREXIA NERVOSA: CAUSES AND CURES

As with other eating disorders, there does not seem to be a clear-cut, single reason why people willingly starve themselves, sometimes to the point of death. The earliest doctors treating anorectics blamed other diseases, witchcraft, bad humors, and heartbreak. Even today, there is a great deal of confusion among the experts as to the causes of and cures for anorexia. This chapter will explore a few of the many factors thought to cause the disease and several of the therapies currently available to help victims of it. Research is still underway, and new findings are emerging.

### THE "STRAIGHT-A" DIETER

Two facts observed by researchers and professionals treating anorectics may be clues to its causes. Nearly all sufferers begin with an overly strict diet, and the vast majority are rated very highly in intelligence tests. Most dieters have trouble sticking to their diets. They consider it a woeful, difficult task, and would rather be eating. In the beginning, the anorectic may feel the same way. But, unlike the typical dieter, the anorectic is impressed with how much weight she initially loses. Soon, she strives to be the best dieter possible, and gets caught up in the starvation syndrome that takes over her life.

Common sense tells us that a "straight-A" student—a high achiever scholastically and in other areas, such as athletics—would be smart enough not to get caught up in a dangerous game like this. But as with any other normal drive, the drive for success can become a distorted obsession. The long-term pressure to always be the best and to hide shortcomings can take its toll. When the pressure becomes too intense, the person may decide that the only thing she can really control is her body. Since being thin is a societal norm, she may find this a logical goal at first, but then get entirely caught up in it. The same healthy drive and intelligence that caused her to become a good student becomes distorted into an obsession.

## HIDDEN PRESSURES

The anorectic often seemed like the perfect young girl to those around her. She caused her parents, friends, and teachers few problems. She worked hard to hide or ignore the negative feelings like frustration, jealousy, loneliness, anger, and fear that most people experience at times.

When she becomes a teenager, she must deal with new uncertainties. Her body is changing and may seem awkward and strange. She faces awakening sexual desires, and sees those around her entering the scary world of dating. The success she has known at home and at school is no longer enough. She is now expected to perform in new ways and face new challenges. One way to deny this change in her body is to starve away the evidence. Many experts believe that the anorectic wishes she could return to the safety of childhood instead of facing the uncertainty that adolescence often brings.

## FEAR OF GROWING UP

Until the last few years, one of the dominant theories was that female anorectics were afraid to face their own sexual development and that their refusal to eat was somehow related to this. It was believed that anorexia was an expression of conflicting emotions about pregnancy and about their relationships with their fathers. More recently, most therapists have come to believe that this is an over-simplification of the many complex family and personal pressures that anorectics face. An anorectic's fear of growing up is only one of many factors that lead to her disease.

## POWER THROUGH STARVING

While an anorectic is obsessed by her disease, she is intensely proud of her emaciation. Although those around her are painfully aware of her failing health and weakening body, she feels like a caterpillar shedding an ugly skin and turning into a butterfly. As she continues her starvation and ignores her hunger pains, she may feel like a religious saint or the most fashionable model. Soon her disease affects her mental state and often intensifies her fantasies.

She sees her skeletal body as evidence of her growing power to transcend the hunger that all human beings feel. At first, she may not be aware of the power her disease has over those around her. By starving, she gets everyone's attention. She can frighten and intimidate others. No family wants the world wondering why their daughter, sister, niece, or cousin is starving. Besides the love and concern they feel for the anorectic, they face a terrible social stigma.

In *Eating Disorders,* Dr. Bruch tells about one anorectic daughter who ordered her parents to keep no food in the house between meals. She asked them to deliver to her the exact meals she requested in order to keep her weight at a low point, and she determined what that weight was.

If her meals were not cooked and served according to her criteria, she threw tantrums, destroyed furniture, and threatened her parents physically. Her family had to move to a secret location to avoid her rage.

Although this is an extreme case, many anorectics demand that their families and friends prove that they care by getting them expensive, exotic food at strange hours of the night. The anorectic's confused state of mind often causes her to exploit the power that her disease has over others. After all, she holds the trump card. If she dies, they will feel responsible.

## BEAUTIFUL SKELETON

Why does the anorectic think her yellowed, broken-out skin, loss of hair, huge, sad eyes, and shaky movements are beautiful? Perhaps it stems from our current societal mania for thinness. As we have seen, American society was not always so obsessed with undernourished body sizes. At the beginning of the twentieth century, women were thought to be beautiful if they had full hips and large breasts.

Researchers have found that people living in countries where famines or depressed economies are common, and where starvation is still a possibility, report little or no cases of anorexia among their populations. Perhaps the availability of food itself makes a big difference in the societal attitudes toward body weight. In many societies where food is not always plentiful, fat bodies are a sign of affluence and good health. In times of deprivation, those with a layer of fat will have some insurance against starvation. Since starvation is not an issue for much of the Western world, dieting amidst an abundance of food becomes a focus instead.

The shrinking size of the ideal woman is seen by many as a reaction to women's political battles for increased rights. One theory is that men who feel threatened by ambitious women feel more at ease around smaller women. Another theory suggests that women themselves want to lose the bulky, nurturing image, so that they can better compete with men by looking more like them.

## FAMILY DYNAMICS

As early as the late seventeenth century, doctors mentioned the influence of the family on anorectic patients. More recent studies have revealed certain characteristics that many of these patients' families have in common. A majority of anorectics come from upper middle-class and wealthy families. Many are born relatively late in their parents' lives and they are often the only or youngest child. They frequently have parents and siblings who are extremely well-educated and who work as professionals, civic leaders, business managers and owners, and in other highly esteemed jobs. Sometimes their mothers are highly-educated, but have sacrificed their careers to raise their children. Often, their fathers are very successful but have little time to spend at home. Some anorectics first start dieting because of a comment about "plumpness" by their mother or father. Sometimes, there is a family history of dieting or an extreme preoccupation with gourmet food or ethnic specialties.

In any family, mealtime is important. Family members have a chance to talk and share their news, plans, and dreams. However, an overprotective mother may force her children to overeat when they are full or not hungry.

A recent article by Eileen Kuperschmid in *The Berkshire Sampler,* "Two Weeks in the Mountains," illustrates the kind of family problem that can lead to an eating disorder.

> *Over coffee, I watched a nearby family of five—a mom, a dad and three kids under the age of five—struggling through their meal.*
>
> *Dad was clearly angry. He swatted the kids, threw angry looks at his wife, shoveled his mashed potatoes into his mouth, and grudgingly cut his daughter's meat into bite-size pieces.*
>
> *"You listen to me," he said to his wife, waving his steak knife in her direction, "and you listen good. Don't you ever tell me what to do again. Do you understand? I can't believe you're actually sitting there and trying to tell me what to do."*
>
> *The woman hung her head. The children looked at their parents, at each other, pushed their food around, kept their mouths shut. This was clearly dangerous ground. Dad was mad and everyone else was scared.*

Family interaction is seen by many therapists as the key issue behind the anorectic's refusal to eat. Other therapists, like Steven Levenkron, see it as only one factor. In his book, *Treating and Overcoming Anorexia Nervosa,* Levenkron refers to the families of anorectics as often being "depleted and exhausted." A child in this kind of family may become independent too early and take on a nurturing role herself although she has not been provided with the nurturing she needs. When this early responsibility becomes too much to bear, she may retreat to childhood by starving herself.

## NO MIRACLE CURES

The many emotional factors that cause anorexia are not easy to combat, especially after the disease has taken over the anorectic's life. The road back to mental and physical health often takes many months or years, and there are numerous setbacks. Although there are no miracle cures, new treatments, many of them developed over the past few decades, are helping thousands of anorectics. The sooner that most victims of this disease receive competent professional help, both medically and psychologically, the better their chances are for recovery. Many recovered anorectics, families of anorectics, therapists, and medical doctors have formed groups such as the American Anorexia Nervosa Association, to help sufferers and their families and friends find the information, help, and support that they need.

## THE MEDICAL PROBLEMS

Anorexia can leave its victim in a critical physical condition. An anorectic may suffer serious injury to her weakened muscles and bones when she exercises them. She may even be on the verge of death, due to chemical imbalances and/or the malfunction of her heart, kidneys, or other vital organs.

A therapist treating a severely emaciated anorectic must walk a careful tightrope. She or he knows that any patient must trust her therapist if treatment is to be successful. In the case of an anorectic, the therapist knows she will distrust anyone trying to suddenly change her medical condition. Yet, this medical condition of starvation causes significant deterioration of mental health. The therapist must not ignore such an extreme physical and mental condition, but must somehow also win the patient's trust. If the medical condition is serious enough, the therapist may have to wait until after medical treatment has begun to introduce meaningful psychological therapy.

Because the physical condition of the anorectic is a critical factor in her emotionally-caused disorder, therapists often team with internists. In this way, the anorectic's delicate physical condition can be monitored.

## HOSPITALIZATION

A medical doctor closely monitoring the anorectic's vital signs may decide her condition is becoming critical. Or, she may collapse. If both a medical doctor and therapist are working with the anorectic, they will consult each other and try to prepare the patient for the hospitalization that is now necessary. This is usually done if the anorectic's weight drops to eighty pounds (36 kg) and she is still losing weight; if she has abnormal blood pressure and heartbeat; or if she is suffering from a slowly healing infection or injury.

Hospitalization removes the anorectic from a home situation that may be fostering or intensifying her problems. A few anorectics, exhausted from their starvation diets and disease, welcome hospitalization. But most are hostile because they see it as a threat to their autonomy. They may desperately try schemes to get out of the hospital, such as telling their parents they are being mistreated. If the hospital does not have specially trained personnel, experienced in dealing with anorectics, the patient may successfully pit nurses, doctors, and attendants against each other, and prevent each from treating her. Since she is no longer in charge of her own food supply, she may hide food or develop new rituals. If she is still able to move on her own, she may pace the floors or become obsessed with helping the other patients. Because their needs are unique, many research and big-city hospitals have developed special wards for the treatment of anorectics.

Usually, entering the hospital does not help the anorectic gain weight. When her condition reaches the critical point, she must be forced to eat. Three methods are used to force nutrition upon an unwilling anorectic: behavior modification and two different types of tube feeding. Behavior modification means the anorectic's behavior—not eating—is changed or modified by a series of rewards and punishments. The patient is given a specific set of weight goals and is told that if she does not reach them, she will lose privileges such as reading, watching TV, exercising, or seeing friends, other patients, and family. Each "contract" between an anorectic and the hospital staff is based on her medical needs and the privileges she values. Often, this kind of contract brings about some immmediate weight gain. But it is also resented by some anorectics, who go back to starving themselves once they have completed its terms. Because of its short-term success and rebound effect, behavior modification is generally used only for critical weight gain, and is usually supplemented by therapy and other forms of medical treatment.

## HYPERALIMENTATION

Until the past few years, the only way to force-feed an anorectic was through the painful, difficult process of inserting a tube down her throat. Anorectics often felt it was a punishment forced upon them for not eating. A bulimic anorectic could also rid herself of the dreaded food soon after she was fed.

A new kind of tube-feeding, developed in the last few years, is called *hyperalimentation*. Its name comes from the combination of "hyper," meaning an excessive amount, and "alimentation," meaning the act or process of supplying or getting nutrition. In surgical procedure, a tube is inserted into a major vein right above the patient's heart, and a liquid containing complete nourishment is sent through the tube into the anorectic's system. Unlike tube-feeding through the throat, the anorectic is unable to regurgitate what she is fed, and this direct absorption allows her to gain weight smoothly and quickly. Since the tube is surgically attached to the chest, near the anorectic's shoulder, she may suffer from stiffness in her shoulder and upper-arm. She may also resent the sound of the electric pump that is monitoring her nutritional intake. But, despite these drawbacks, it is a much more humane and effective way to force-feed an anorectic.

While hyperalimentation is reviving her depleted body, the anorectic's therapist can concentrate on helping her to develop a healthy attitude toward eating. As she becomes able to eat on her own, hyperalimentation can be adjusted or discontinued.

## GETTING TO THE HEART
## OF THE PROBLEM

While it is possible to heal the anorectic's body, it is often more difficult to alter her pattern of starvation and to help her cope with the mental dilemmas behind it. Many anorectics, supposedly cured when they regain their lost weight, resort to bulimic practices or become anorectic again.

An anorectic needs an in-depth program of psychological assistance to help her examine the reasons behind her illness, and to prevent its recurrence. Traditional psychiatry and psychotherapy offer this kind of help, but each is a gradual process that takes several months or years. Because anorectics need immediate help, traditional methods of therapy have been combined with or replaced by techiniques developed specially for dealing with anorectics.

In *The Golden Cage*, Dr. Hilde Bruch uses one of her patient's images to illustrate the lack of self-esteem at the heart of many anorectics' problems. The anorectic patient describes herself as feeling like a "sparrow in a golden cage, too plain and simple for the luxuries of her home, but also deprived of the freedom of doing what she truly wanted to do."

The therapist must try to help the anorectic develop a better self-image. Dr. Bruch describes therapy as "an attempt to repair the conceptual defects and distortions, the deep-seated sense of dissatisfaction and isolation, and the conviction of incompetence" that anorectics feel.

## FAMILY THERAPY

In family therapy, an anorectic can examine her role in the family, and see her interaction with other members in new and different ways. Since the anorectic's disease is so severe, it is bound to affect the entire family. Therefore, it is important to deal with their frustrations, anger, and guilt, if the anorectic is going to return to her family home or interact with family members.

One group of psychotherapists sees the family as the primary "system" influencing the anorectic's behavior. They feel that it is essential for other family members to first examine and then try to improve their interactions with each other. Since the family is seen as a "system," one individual is rarely blamed for the anorectic's problems.

In the book, *Psychosomatic Families,* Salvador Minuchin and other therapists explain how family therapy helps the anorectic's entire family change and grow.

*. . . a girl who had hitherto presented herself as helpless and hopeless, dominated and invaded by her mother, could now be seen as tyrannically manipulating her intimidated parents. A father whose dearest wish was to have his child eat and grow healthy again could be seen as undercutting his wife's efforts in this direction.*

Family therapists say that this method requires less time in order to help the anorectic improve. Her home environment improves as she does. Critics of family therapy say that it is no substitute for the examination of the anorectic's personal problems, and that many family members have such intense problems of their own, or fears of psychotherapy, that it is often impossible to get their cooperation.

## HELPING EACH OTHER
Recovering and recovered anorectics can offer another troubled victim relief from her isolation. Many groups for anorectics are started by therapists who realize the importance of interaction between their patients. Others are started by recovering anorectics themselves who want to help others.

Since many college students suffer from eating disorders, groups are often formed on campus. One such group was formed during the 1981–82 school year at Williams College. Over forty people showed up at the first meeting. A smaller number of people attended further meetings, and an ongoing group emerged.

Exploratory groups like the one at Williams College allow the anorectic to view herself more clearly. They offer her a chance to confide in others who understand what she is facing.

Although most therapists feel that group interaction can be an important part of an anorectic's recovery process, many caution against using it as a substitute for personal, in-depth psychotherapy, or as an alternative to seeking medical help. Some therapists feel that unless binging and purging bulimics are separated from anorectics not using bulimic practices, anorectics may learn bulimic habits.

## THE NURTURANT-
## AUTHORITATIVE APPROACH

A relatively new, very promising therapy for helping anorectics is called the nurturant-authoritative approach. Developed by Steven Levenkron, it is based on his twelve years of experience successfully treating many anorectics.

Levenkron's approach is different from standard practice, which is rather passive and allows the patient to deal with his or her own problems without much intervention from the therapist. Often, anorectics need a special kind of support and firmness to find the courage to defeat their disease.

In nurturant-authoritative psychotherapy, the therapist is both nurturant and authoritative toward the patient. Nurturant refers to the supportive, warm attitude that a therapist must provide. This produces an atmosphere of love and trust. At the same time, the therapist maintains an authoritative role. That is, he or she firmly insists that the patient change her behavior so she can free herself from the disease.

The combination of authority and nurturing creates a solid, parent-like manner which is intended to give the anorectic the kind of support she has not had in her family life. In therapy, the patient regresses back to childhood, and then "grows up" again with the support and guidance of her therapist.

In his second book, *Treating and Overcoming Anorexia Nervosa,* Levenkron fully explains his approach.

The nurturant-authoritative technique demands more emotional involvement from the therapist than traditional methods. But the anorectic in this case is often much more difficult to treat. Levenkron explains the extra burden of his approach as follows:

> *A nurturant-authoritative psychotherapy demands more initiative, more tactical decision making, and more varied, deliberate behavior on the part of the therapist than does traditional therapy. . . The therapist takes the explicit role of a helping person who has ways of guiding the patient out of her lonely and pathological state.*

The philosophy of this approach goes against the flexibility and lack of specific direction frequently found in other methods of therapy. The therapist must take responsibility for a patient who is often in a critical physical state. For these reasons, and many more, there has been considerable initial resistance to this new approach. It has proved to be much more effective than former approaches though, and therapists are now using it a great deal. Proponents say it has been at least 85 percent effective in producing a *real* cure in anorectics.

## THE RAINBOW'S END

Most cures take at least a few months, even in the most optimistic of cases, and a majority take several years, with periods of regression. Still, therapists who have helped many anorectics claim the long fight is worth it. Dr. Bruch describes the therapist's reaction to an anorectic's recovery in her book, *The Golden Cage:* "There is nothing more rewarding than seeing these narrow, rigid, isolated creatures change into warm, spontaneous human beings with a wide range of interests and an active participation in life."

Anorexia is only one of the many kinds of food abuse that trick and trap people. Perhaps the increased publicity about compulsive eating, bulimia, and anorexia, and the great amount of dedicated research and intense therapy currently being conducted will help reduce the epidemic of food abuse. More importantly, perhaps these phenomena will help each victim find the kind of emotionally-rewarding, complete life that she or he deserves.

# FOR FURTHER INFORMATION AND READING

The following is a list of research centers and institutions offering help and information, and support groups. Most of the organizations and institutions rely on donations, grants, and other contributions for their functioning. When writing to them, enclose a large, self-addressed envelope with twice the current first-class postage attached.

## RESEARCH GROUPS AND INSTITUTIONS OFFERING THERAPY

Eating Disorders Project, Michael Reese Hospital and Medical Center, 2959 Cottage Grove, Chicago, IL 60616, 312—791-3878.

Behavioral Health Clinic, Department of Adult Psychiatry, University of Minnesota Hospital, 420 Delaware St. S.E., Box 301 MAYO, Minneapolis, MN 55455, 612—376-9166.

The Center for the Study of Anorexia and Bulimia, Institute For Contemporary Psychotherapy, 1 West 91st St., New York, NY 10024, 212—595-3449.

Eating Disorders Program, Neuropsychiatric Institute, UCLA Hospital and Clinics, University of California, Los Angeles, CA 90024, 213—825-0173.

Eating Disorders Program, New York Hospital, Cornell University Medical Center, Westchester Division, 21 Bloomingdale Rd., White Plains, NY 10605, 914—682-9100.

Eating Disorders Research and Treatment Program, New York State Psychiatric Institute, Columbia Presbyterian Medical Center, 722 W. 168th St., New York, NY 10032, 212—960-5747.

The Eating and Weight Disorder Clinic, Henry Phipps Psychiatric Clinic, Johns Hopkins Hospital, 600 N. Wolfe St., Baltimore, MD 21205, 301—955-5790.

## SUPPORT GROUPS

**Georgia:** American Anorexia Nervosa Association of Atlanta, 3533 Kingsboro Rd. N.E., Atlanta, GA 30319, 404—266-8779.

**Illinois, Nationwide, and Canada:** National Association of Anorexia Nervosa and Associated Disorders (ANAD), Box 271, Highland Park, IL 60035, 312—831-3438.

There are more than 90 affiliated ANAD groups in 35 states and Canada. Contact ANAD for the group nearest you. ANAD also provides educational materials for schools. Schools should send $1.00 for postage. Do not include an envelope.

**Massachusetts:** Anorexia Nervosa Aid Society of Massachusetts, Inc., Box 213, Lincoln, MA 01773, 617–259-9767.

**New Jersey and Nationwide:** American Anorexia Nervosa Association, 133 Cedar Lane, Teaneck, NJ 07666, 201—836-1800.

**Ohio:** National Anorexic Aid Society, P.O. Box 29461 Coral Road, Columbus, OH 43229, 614—846-6810.

**Pennsylvania:** American Anorexia Nervosa Association of Philadelphia, Philadelphia Child Guidance Clinic, Philadelphia, PA 19104, 215—387-1919.

**Virginia:** American Anorexia Nervosa Association of Tidewater Virginia, c/o Riverside Hospital Community Mental Health Center, 420 J. Clyde Morris Blvd., Newport News, VA 23601, 804—599-2100.

## BOOKS

Bruch, Hilde. *Eating Disorders: Obesity, Anorexia Nervosa, and The Person Within.* Basic Books: New York, 1973.

Bruch, Hilde. *The Golden Cage: The Enigma of Anorexia Nervosa.* Harvard University Press: Cambridge, 1978.

Chernin, Kim. *The Obsession—Reflections on The Tyranny of Slenderness.* Harper & Row: New York, 1981.

Fonda, Jane. *Jane Fonda's Workout Book.* Simon and Schuster: New York, 1981.

Levenkron, Steven. *The Best Little Girl in The World.* Warner: New York, 1979.

Levenkron, Steven. *Treating and Overcoming Anorexia Nervosa.* Scribners: New York, 1982.

Orbach, Susie. *Fat Is a Feminist Issue.* Paddington Press: New York, 1978.

Sours, John A. *Starving to Death in a Sea of Objects: The Anorexia Nervosa Syndrome.* Aronson: New York, 1980.

## MAGAZINE ARTICLES, PAMPHLETS, AND NEWSLETTERS

The American Anorexia Nervosa Association Newsletter.

Brody, Jane E. "Anorexia Nervosa, An Ailment Rising Among Teenage Girls, Is Yielding to a New Therapy." *New York Times,* July 14, 1982.

The Center For The Study of Anorexia and Bulimia. *The Eating Disorder Bulimia.* New York: Institute For Contemporary Psychotherapy, 1982.

Ibid, *Anorexia Nervosa,* 1982.

"Eating Binges: Anorexia's Sister Ailment." *Time.* November 17, 1980.

Kintzing, Jennifer M. "What the Experts Say About Anorexia Nervosa." *Seventeen.* July, 1982.

Marks, Judi, "Disturbed Eating Habits." *Teen.* October, 1981.

McCoy, Kathy. "Are You Obsessed with Your Weight?" *Seventeen.* July, 1982.

Woods, Jennifer. "I Was Starving Myself to Death." *Mademoiselle.* May, 1981.

Stein, Margery Beth. "The Eating Disorder Women Don't Talk About." *McCall's.* August, 1981.

# INDEX